"WOO completely ~~~~~ ~~~ ~~~~
Dr. Kenda Creasy Dean
Author, *Almost Christian*

WOO

AWAKENING TEENAGERS' DESIRE TO FOLLOW IN THE WAY OF JESUS

Thank you for loving + serving students!

Morgan Schmidt

MORGAN SCHMIDT

Morgan Schmidt is a snappy and relatable writer. But above all, she is a prophet blessed with a winsome honesty that sneaks up on you as you're planning your umpteenth mission trip and whispers: "*Recalculate.*" For Schmidt, being human boils down to desire; and youth ministry that's honest is about desire too—the desires of youth for God, the desire of God for them. With *Woo*, Morgan Schmidt joins a new class of practical theologians taking aim at the false gods driving the youth ministry industry, and she restores our focus—and our hope—on young people's God-given desire to become, belong to, and worship as the body of Christ. *Woo* completely won me over.

Kenda Creasy Dean, Mary D. Synnott Professor of Youth, Church and Culture at Princeton Theological Seminary and author of Almost Christian: What the Faith of Our Teenagers Is Telling the American Church

Woo is, hands down, one of the most sensible and simultaneously exhilarating books about pastoring students that I have read in a long time. Morgan Schmidt wisely guides us to awaken desire rather than run from it, equipping us to form desire to follow in the way of Jesus. *Woo* invites leaders to see students as real people, with real longings that matter. Don't let the warmth and wit of Morgan's writing fool you—this changes everything you've known about youth ministry.

Dwight J. Friesen, Associate Professor of Practical Theology @ The Seattle School of Theology & Psychology, coauthor of The New Parish

Woo is a book about desire, the desire of young people to be authentic and real. It is also about the desire for those who serve the Church to be the midwives who help them do just that. Knowing Morgan Schmidt, I can tell you this book is authentic and real. Here is offered one devoted person's theology and praxis around the ministry to youth. I highly recommend it, and I thank God for this offering to the Church.

The Rt. Rev. Gregory H. Rickel, VIII, Bishop of Olympia

Both Augustine and Kierkegaard, in their own ways, asserted that we are what we desire. Consumerism has adopted in a counterfeit but powerful way this theology. When our desires go askew and latch onto consumer goods, political ideologies, or fear about our children, we create pantheons of idols to worship. Like a prophet from the Old Testament, Morgan Schmidt has called out youth ministry for its idol-making, asserting with flare and depth that youth ministry has been captured by desires other than encountering the living God. This is a book that will challenge you because it will ask you to expose your desires. But in so doing, you may find not the idol of successful youth ministry, but the living God who will draw you closer and closer to the humanity of young people this living God loves.

Dr. Andrew Root, Luther Seminary

I really like what Morgan Schmidt is saying to youth pastors in *Woo: Awakening Teenagers' Desire to Follow in the Way of Jesus*. We should know by now that approaching the Christian formation of young people in our churches needs something more than doubling down on what we think worked in the past or even a "new" method or model—a full theological paradigmatic shift is necessary. Morgan carefully unveils a more spiritual posture toward the young people we want to do life with. It starts with a passion to approach them with a sense of awe in their personhood. It involves our curiosity and commitment to cooperate with the Holy Spirit's work of unleashing a young person's imagination in the pursuit of discovering his or her beautiful God-given humanity. Maybe if we spent more time nourishing our own lives with God and what it means for us to become more fully human, we might just find ourselves around young people who feel fully alive desiring life in Jesus Christ. If you are comfortably ensconced in a church that puts on programs for youth to consume, and measures its success based on immediate results—don't read this book. It will either make you very uncomfortable or—if it captures you—it could get you fired. But, then again, it could also spark an awakening in your congregation.

Mike King, President/CEO of Youthfront, author of Presence-Centered Youth Ministry: Guiding Students into Spiritual Formation. *Follow MDKing on Twitter.*

Woo: Awakening Teenagers' Desire to Follow in the Way of Jesus

Copyright © 2014 by Morgan Schmidt

Publisher: Mark Oestreicher
Managing Editor: Laura Gross
Cover Design & Layout: Adam McLane
Creative Director: Dale Carnegie

ISBN-13: 978-0-9910050-2-4
ISBN-10: 0991005023

The Youth Cartel, LLC
www.theyouthcartel.com

Email: info@theyouthcartel.com

Born in San Diego
Printed in the U.S.A.

This book is for my students,
but it's because of Ian.

I want to write something
So simply
about love
or about pain
that even
as you are reading
you feel it
and as you read
you keep feeling it
and though it be my story
it will be common,
though it be singular
it will be known to you
so that by the end
you will think—
no, you will realize—
that it was all the while
yourself arranging the words,
that it was all the time
words that you yourself,
out of your heart
had been saying.

—Mary Oliver, *Evidence*

CONTENTS

A WORD FROM THE PUBLISHER

Publishing is tough these days. (I wanted to write, "It's gettin' hard out here for a pimp," but I thought the music/movie reference might get lost, and some would be offended.) Most publishers just cannot afford to release a book by an author who doesn't have a built-in platform to move thousands of copies on her own.

Morgan Schmidt does *not* have a platform to move thousands of copies of this book on her own.

But, call us visionary or passionate or stupid, we simply had to publish Morgan's book. Morgan Schmidt is more than the ideas and words on these pages; we believe she's an important emerging voice in youth ministry. And built into the DNA of The Youth Cartel is a commitment to find people like Morgan and help them shape all of us.

And the words on these pages—well, I am really not blowing smoke when I write that they are among the most important and reorienting and revolutionary and fresh words written about youth ministry in the last couple years. Plus, as a bonus, Morgan writes in a winsome way that leaves you no choice but to really like her, whether you agree with her proposals and perspectives and time-delayed explosives or not. As with most of the stuff we publish or host at our events, our goal at The Youth Cartel is not that you agree with us (or fall prey to our megalomaniacal plans to rule the world), but that you are invited to think, reflect, and hear the voice of God about youth ministry.

With that, I'm excited to introduce you to *Woo: Awakening Teenagers' Desire to Follow in the Way of Jesus* and to the insightful Morgan Schmidt. (You can take it from here, Morgan…)

Mark Oestreicher
Partner | The Youth Cartel

ACKNOWLEDGEMENTS

Much love and many thanks to those who made this book a reality:

Laura Gross, editor extraordinaire

Mark Oestreicher, Adam McLane, and The Youth Cartel for instigating a revolution

Paul Martin, for reading me well

Tim Soerens and Paul Sparks, for inviting me into the parish

Dwight Friesen, for teaching me to be a pastor

Rev. Peter Strimer, for cheering me on

St. Andrew's Episcopal Church, for painting my office teal

Mom, for always believing in me and for not asking how the book is coming along

Danny, for believing in me and trying all of my crazy schemes

Toby the Dog, for being my pastor, therapist, and friend

Ian, for being my person and showing me unspeakably generous love

INTRODUCTION

This is the note that ruined me, in a good way.

Chris, an eighth grade boy whom I'd pastored for three years, wrote me this letter when I transitioned out of being his youth pastor. He's really amazing, one of those kids who make you think, *One day I'll get to say I was his youth pastor!*

Morgan,

I have thoroughly enjoyed the past three years. You have never failed to bring life into even the tiniest of things, whether it be an idea as simple as ice blocking, or something as sophisticated as attempting to explain the significance of heaven. Despite all the cracks that break the earth, you always find a place of life, where things grow and thrive.

This, I think, is how you've shown me God is here, today, working to mend these cracks. You lit another candle—and not your routine candle which you light each week. You lit a candle in my soul.

Though I must admit I struggle, for that little light often wavers from the cruel winds of this broken world, I must say thank you for planting that wonderful seed of faith. I do hope that youth group, as well as myself, has helped you in a similar way. I hope we have helped you to grow in a way you did not expect, to gain insight that will be good news to you in the future.

Once again, thank you, and may God be with you.

Chris

Four years ago I had the rare opportunity to build a youth ministry from scratch. The community was a blank slate, a tantalizing chance to practice being with students in the way I had always dreamed, free of the expectations that come with history. My students and I learned alongside each other how to bring our whole selves and our desires to bear on our faith, in conversation and in meaningful action.

The challenging thing about youth ministry is that we really only know how we're doing in hindsight. In the midst of doing life with students, we don't always get to see how students continue following in the way of Jesus.

Chris's note made me think that maybe we'd created something truly formational and good together over the years, and it had something to do with encouraging students to show up with their whole selves.

We found each other to be so good.
We found that God believes we are good, too.
And it all revolves around desire.

I didn't have the words for it when we started. Using the label of *desire* is entirely my husband's fault because Ian sees human behavior through a lens of what people want. Together, we learned to put language to the ways in which people do what they want; and if what they want is connected to good things, then they will keep doing good things.

There are versions of the Christian narrative that might say this is self-serving, that we're not meant to do what *we* want (even if it's good), but we should only do what *God* wants. This is the same story that insists God should use us for God's purposes, whether we like it or not.

We don't use the people we love. And if God is love, then God

is not in the business of using people either. St. Irenaeus said, "The glory of God is [a human being] fully alive."[1] Our reason for being isn't to go to Siberia just because we think God can use us there. Frederick Buechner insisted that "our vocation is where our greatest passion meets the world's greatest need."
.

Naming desire made everything click. Students might continue wrestling with their faith and doubts; and they might continue participating in the work of the kingdom, if we can help them *want* it. This book is the expression of a dream and a vision, a new way of forming and loving students by believing they are good and paying attention to their desires.

Since this book is about desire and since youth workers care about people, I'd like to tell you a few things about myself that might put the rest of the book in better context for us.

I love youth ministry and always want to be a youth pastor. I'm a practitioner at heart with little patience for academia or anything that I can't apply to real life.

I am a woman. My name can go either way, I know, and this has led to some really awkward phone interviews with churches who like my résumé but dislike my gender.

After running in evangelical circles since my junior high days, I've become an Episcopalian. Yes, Episcopalians have youth pastors. I am falling in love with progressive theology and ancient liturgy all at the same time.

I speak about God without using male pronouns (which you'll notice throughout this book), and it's taken a while for me to break that habit. I know it sounds awkward sometimes. And I don't mean to imply that God is a lady. I just really love the idea that God contains the fullness of both genders, and I lament the fact that the English language denies us a neuter pronoun that would be more appropriate than *it*.

Everything in this book is for you, too. Good news is for you as much as it's for your students.

This is not a finished work. Just as I believe the story of God and humanity continues to unfold beyond the pages of Scripture, so I hope we will wrestle with these words and continue the conversation beyond this book.

Together may we keep inviting ourselves, our students, and the church to live into the desire to follow in the way of Jesus and participate in the ongoing creation of the kingdom of God.

1

WOULD YOU RATHER? DESIRE

I'm in love with a commercial for a cell phone service provider. There are different versions of it, but the tagline is "It's not complicated. _____ is better." Apparently this company has faster downloads or something. I don't know. They're not my carrier. I just like their ads.

The brand spokesman is sitting in a classroom with a group of six-year-olds, and he's asking them an earnest question about what they want. As you picture this, please know that this guy is taking these kids completely and wonderfully seriously.

> Spokesman: "What's better, faster or slower?"
> Kids: "FASTER!"
> Spokesman: "And what's fast?"
> Kid 1: "Um, my mom's car and a cheetah."
> Spokesman: "Okay."
> Kid 2: "A spaceship!"
> Spokesman: "A spaceship. What's slow?"
> Kid 3: "My grandma's slow."
> Spokesman: "Would you like her better if she was fast?"
> Kid 3: "I bet she would like it if she was fast."

Spokesman: "Hmm. Maybe give
her some turbo-boosters."
Kid 3: "Or tape a cheetah to her back."
Spokesman: "Tape a cheetah to her back? Seems like
you've thought about this before."

Cue the jingle about how it's not complicated—faster is better.
Yay! Faster cell phone service!
But this is not the point.

Brilliant advertising does something. It helps us tap into
our most uninhibited desires. This ad is genius because
with relatively little scripting, these kids' honest desires are
articulated, honored, and then used to sell a product. Except for
the manipulative capitalist part, this is youth ministry.

At our best, the church reveals teenagers' true desires and
connects those longings to bigger stories.

The stories of their lives.
The stories of their communities.
The stories of God.

Would You Rather? is one of my favorite games to play with
students. If you haven't played it before, you should try it. It's
a blast. The gist of it is someone poses an either/or question,
and then everybody shares which choice they'd pick and why.
Pretty simple. You can play it anywhere. Everyone gets to play.
And there are no wrong answers. It's all about desire.

Play it with me for a moment, and you'll see what I mean. Be
honest. Allow yourself to imagine that whatever your answer
is, it's good.

Would you rather go to church or play outside with friends?

Would you rather pray or listen to a new album by your favorite artist?

Would you rather follow a God who delights in you or makes you feel ashamed?

Would you rather be considered a bad person or a good person?

Would you rather wait to get to heaven when you die or experience heaven on earth?

Would you rather do what you want or do what's expected of you?

Would you rather be coerced into caring for someone or love them because you want to?

If you chose the options you really wanted, then you're a human being. As much as we possibly can, we humans do what we want. If you *didn't* choose the options you really wanted, that's okay too. You're still a human being. Many of us have become very, very good at denying what we want in order to please others or be viewed as "right."

My bet is you chose whichever response seemed good to you. Even if you lied, you lied because it seemed like it would be good to do so.

People want good things.
Yet goodness is in the eye of the desirer.
The idea of what's "good" changes from person to person.
And what we desire defines us.

If you are a youth pastor, what do you want when it comes to your work with students?

When people ask why you're a youth worker, what do you say?

There's a story about a shepherd who loses one of her sheep. She immediately leaves the flock and goes after the wanderer. When she finds the lost sheep, she carries him home rejoicing. We're told this story is one of many about how God interacts with humanity. God is the Seeker and Finder of lost things. Following in the way of Jesus means looking for the lost and celebrating the found. The tough part is discerning which is which. If we're talking about lost and found people, sinners and saints, it would be easier if we all wore identifying jerseys. If only Jesus had left us some sort of "What kind of sheep are you?" survey to share on social media.

Along with passages like the Great Commission, this story about the lost sheep is often taken as an evangelical imperative. Jesus' message seems clear: Do whatever you have to do to get the wayward soul back to the flock.

Youth ministry has taken this task very seriously and creatively. No other ministry of the church can boast going to such lengths to bring people to faith. We will do just about anything to get kids in the door—and even more to keep them there.

We want so badly to find them.

We make videos, play popular music, organize skits, make jokes, play games, eat pizza, go on trips, and meet on a weeknight instead of on Sunday mornings. There is only one problem: all of the latest research on adolescence and spirituality suggests that our creative, high-tech, jam-packed programs aren't working.

Conservative estimates say that 60 percent of young people who were involved in a youth group will abandon their faith once they leave home. All sorts of thoughtful people have written about this phenomenon: Christian Smith, Kenda Creasy Dean, David Kinnaman, and Mark Oestreicher, to name a few. (And I highly recommend their works to you.[2])

Sixty percent of our students don't have a faith they want to keep once they graduate from high school. More than half of our students don't want what the church has offered them. In an effort to figure out why, David Kinnaman has conducted hundreds of interviews with kids who left the church. They see the church as:

Overprotective
Shallow
Anti-science
Repressive
Exclusive
Doubtless (not a place where they can express their doubts and ask questions)
Not a place where they encounter God[3]

This is terrifying news for youth workers, parents, pastors, and faith communities. As a church, we think we can fix the situation by frantically creating bigger and flashier programs, building special youth spaces, or hiring a cooler youth worker.

And as a youth pastor, sometimes I feel like if I could just get my hands on the right book, go to the right conference, read the right blogs, or join the right network, I would finally figure out how to keep the church from bleeding out.

Our fears caused this exodus in the first place—fear of sin, doubt, bad behavior, and popular culture. Some of us are terrified our students will go to hell if they don't accept Jesus into their hearts. Others are afraid they'll end up pregnant—or worse, they might have sex.

Youth ministry is a failed experiment in behavior modification. We've created youth ministries that simply serve to keep kids happy, nice, safe, and sex-free. We're helicopter youth pastors hovering over our students' souls so they won't miss a step. Nowhere in the Bible does it say that Jesus came to make us nice and abstinent.

Jesus came that we might have life, and have it to the full.

When did we decide that life was about always being happy, always being safe, always being nice, and not even thinking about sex until you're married?

Where did we lose hope in the vulnerability of doubt, the opportunity of failure, the preciousness of grief, the certainty of heaven, and the pleasure of sex?

I'm using the church's sex education strategy as a microcosm, since abstinence is such a central part of Christian youth culture. Can you imagine what might happen if, when we spoke to students about their sexuality, we talked about how they could be awesome, whole, sexual beings? Can you picture their faces if you stood up and said, "Sex is awesome. Sex can be awesome for you, too. Here's how . . . " and then you spoke about loving our own bodies; respecting others' bodies; what it means to be a whole woman or man; how unsatisfying, unhealthy, and heartbreaking sex is when it happens outside a committed relationship; and how it's God's dream that we have that sexual experience with someone who loves us so much that he or she wants to marry us and be with us for the rest of our lives? Oh, and if you fail? God still loves you, the church still loves you, and you're not "ruined" or "tainted" for the rest of your life.

I can't tell you how many Christian college students I've worked with who've gotten married and then freaked out about sex. They're blindsided by the crushing expectation that this activity which was evil only yesterday is now good, expected, and perfect. It's hard to go from zero to sixty, from evil to bliss, when you've been told your whole life that sex is bad.

Instead of a gospel of fear and a sexual ethic of shame, we could offer our students guidance on how to live the best lives ever, while we honor the way God wired them to want good things.

How did the church become an inhospitable place for the goodness of human desire?

Teenagers recognize something desirable when they see it, and they aren't seeing it at church. After all, three out of five students will walk away from their faith altogether.

I clearly remember my reactions when I was first exposed to these statistics:

a. *Freak out.* How can this be? We have all of these youth ministry conferences, books, blogs, and professional youth pastors! If this were a regular business situation, we'd all lose our jobs, and security would escort us to our cars holding our boxes of shame. Seriously. If the local high school graduated only 30 or 40 percent of its students, no one would question that things really need to change.

b. *Sweet relief.* I'm not the only one, thank God. Tara, Ethan, Katie, Clara, Erica, Matt, Brian, Kasey, Rachel, Michelle, and so many more . . . I can name my 60 percent, and I bet you can too.

c. *Sadness bordering on despair.* What more can I do? This is heartbreaking. That 60 percent statistic is so many students. I missed them somehow . . . what could I have done differently? Why do I even bother? Maybe I should just give all of our youth ministry funding to the Boys and Girls Club so it will actually make a difference. And then I cried.

d. *Try to be better.* My final and lasting reaction is to figure out another way. These kids are too important for me to cling to the way I've always done things and be content with missing more than half of them. We should be losing sleep because these are *lives*, not statistics.

I'm not upset because they'll go to hell or have sex. I'm confident that God is still with them and that the Spirit is still at work in all the goodness, beauty, and love their lives hold. I'm also confident that premarital sex is not a death sentence and they will figure out relationships and sexuality as imperfectly as the rest of us have.

These ~~statistics~~ lives matter to me because all of these students are missing out on the reality of the kingdom here and now. Whatever version of the gospel or church or Jesus we presented them with, it simply didn't resonate with them as being good news.

We missed each other.

The church's ministry to youth is broken, and the problem isn't that congregations are shrinking or we aren't meeting our evangelism quotas. The problem is that whole generations are disconnected from God and the unfolding reality of the kingdom. They don't get that the good news is *for them*, that God is *with them, for them*, and crazy *about them* because we aren't speaking about it in a language that matters and connects to what students love.

They don't see how Jesus makes a difference. They don't believe the Spirit is still at work making everything that's broken whole again. And they certainly don't believe they're invited to join God in the restoration of all things. They look at the church and think, *There is no good news here.*

I believe people do what they want.

Teenagers are people. So as far as it's within their power, teenagers will do what they want.

Our desires shape who we are and how we live, so we become what we desire.

If Jesus is connected to what we desire, then we'll keep desiring Jesus.

And if we want to follow Jesus, then we'll become more *like* Jesus.

So youth ministry should be about caring about what teenagers want and connecting their desires to Jesus. At our best, we cultivate adolescents' desire to be like Jesus.

If students found the good news to actually be *good*, then they might want it—and keep wanting it. We wouldn't even have to bribe them with candy.

Can you imagine playing our Would You Rather? game with the average teenager? They'd choose listening to Macklemore or the latest boy band over prayer almost every time. But it's not because they hate talking to God. Most of the time the church asks students to deny their desires, to embrace a faith that degrades the things they love in favor of dead religious obligation.

We can't take the easy way out by blaming our students, the American culture, social media, iPhones, or "big church." Sure, some students will return to the denominations of their youth when they start their own families, and that will be great. But who and what will get lost in the gap? We need to figure out another way of being churches and youth pastors who help students cultivate a sustainable faith that will bend and flex as they continue to grow.

The thing about youth ministry is that, despite all of our training and conferences and books, we still look like we did 40 years ago. This isn't totally evil. It's just that a couple of things have changed since then—like, everything—and this includes youth culture and adolescent desires.

There are many reasons we've stalled. Youth worker burnout and turnover is notorious. We have a very short life expectancy in this field. Sometimes I feel like churches see me as some sort of mythical creature: A female youth pastor with 10 years of experience? What is this sorcery?

A beloved core of veteran saints have stuck around to teach aspiring youth pastors the ways they did youth ministry, and we're so grateful for them. We have to start somewhere, and it's good to listen to the wisdom of those who've gone before us.

The trouble is, most young youth workers don't stay in ministry long enough to modify and adapt the things they've learned in a way that is meaningful to them and to the particular community in which they find themselves. They get frustrated. They burn out. They leave or get tired of being asked when they're going to get a "real" ministry job or become senior pastors.

Senior pastors still remember how they spent a few years doing youth ministry a couple of decades ago. So they want the ambitious, young youth pastors they hire to do exactly what they did back in the day. Their youth ministry experiences now glow with warm nostalgia, and they don't remember how truly pointless and horrifying it was to swallow a live goldfish onstage during a youth retreat. (Why did anyone ever do this?) We have noble mission statements that don't indict poor goldfish. They're all a little different, but the consistent message is that we want to form students so they'll have faith in God. Faith formation falls under two broad categories, depending on which corner of the church world you're from: Evangelical or mainline.

Evangelicals get creative. Every few years we get a new kind of youth ministry model:

Purpose-driven youth ministry
Incarnational youth ministry
Relational youth ministry
Family-centered youth ministry
Presence-centered youth ministry
Ancient-future youth ministry
Postmodern youth ministry

We have deep anxiety that we're not doing enough. That we need to do more. That if we can just figure out the right way to do ministry, then the kids will have faith, the elders will increase our budget, and parents will send us only nice emails.

Every few years, I pray to God that the next ministry trend will be the magic bullet that eases my fear that I am irrelevant and have no idea what I'm doing. Every year the youth ministry books and conferences make me feel worse—like I'll never be enough. And that's because we pile a lot of extras onto the idea of being in relationship with students.

The relational part of these big ideas is very good—doing life with students is sacred work. But the problem is we put all of our energy into building relationships without helping students articulate their experiences of God. This leaves students feeling warm and fuzzy about youth group without internalizing what they believe about God. Then these precious relationships that connected them to Jesus and gave them their spiritual identities are reduced to Likes on a Facebook page soon after high school graduation.

On the other end of the ecclesial spectrum, mainline churches prefer to do faith formation through doctrinal education and poorly explained sacraments. These students tend to really know their stuff; they can articulate theological concepts, ancient creeds, and religious language. There's just one problem: The vast majority of kids *hate* it. Most participate out of obligation or parental coercion. They leave church knowing all the right answers, and that's about it.

There is a lot of good to both of these approaches—or else we wouldn't continue doing them. But as they are generally practiced, they don't serve students or churches well in the long run. On their own, they don't cultivate a sustainable faith.

Why? Because for most students, church hasn't been a place to desire—let alone love—God. Both of these pedagogies leave students on their own, to stumble into loving God with little or no help from the church.

This might sound pretty grim. And it's even more heartbreaking because so much goodness is possible when we tune in to students' desires. There *is* a better way.

We already want to give students what they want, right? So since desire is specific to individuals and communities, the trick is to pay attention and ask what they want.

It's like those helpful yet terrible documentaries about how most of our food is made from chemicals and fillers. The people who make the food defend themselves, saying, "It's what people want; it's what sells." Meanwhile, I'm yelling at the TV that what I actually want is REAL food: happy chickens and cows that get little massages before they're humanely put to sleep and then slaughtered with honor and prayers of gratitude. Is that too much to ask?

In the grand scheme of things, my youth group is comparatively small in number. A few students have told me they skipped one of our gatherings to go check out a bigger youth group in our city. I bless them and tell them I really hope they find whatever they're looking for. But they usually come back. One eighth grade boy even said to me, "There were a lot more kids there. But we just ran around, and they threw balls at me during the games. They think they know what teenagers want, but we didn't even get to talk. No one wanted to have a conversation with me."

Whatever our particular ministry looks like, whether we are parachurch, rural church, megachurch, or mainline;
serve a dozen students or a hundred;
teach a series or follow the lectionary,
meet in small groups, house groups, or big groups;
have a stage or just a few old couches;
get paid a lot, enough, or not at all—
we live for the same moments.

We do what we do because we can't imagine anything better than encountering heaven on earth with our students and watching them discover that the gospel is actually good news. For them. Right now.

Sometimes these moments are specifically about God. Sometimes they are profound glimpses of self-awareness and growth where the students are becoming more and more themselves. Sometimes they are conversations of shared heartache and lament.

But these moments are always good.
When our good desires connect with the ways God is restoring the world, we are never the same.

I have a confession to make: The vast majority of my hours aren't spent on these formational moments. It takes a lot of time to create opportunities for meaningful things to happen. Relentless emailing of parents has to happen. Permission slips have to happen. Fundraising—well, I'm not sure that task is as necessary as we make it out to be, but it sure feels like it most days. We do these things because they allow us to be present with our students and their families when it matters most.

Out of nowhere a student will text me about how he isn't getting along with his stepmom, and he'll ask if I have any ideas about what he should do. I have the indescribable privilege of reminding him that he is good, he is loved, and he has a chance to respond to his family in a way that invites God's presence and restores relationships.

The most meaningful, transformative, formational moments for students—the ones that stick with them—are rarely planned and seldom predicted. The real ah-ha moments are a paradox: the product of intentional serendipity. They simply happen— just like we'd hoped and prayed and expected them to happen.

We don't need more or better programs, songs, retreats, curricula, or small groups. We must become the sort of pastors who invite students into the presence of God with the fullness of their desires, so they'll want to follow in the way of Jesus beyond youth group.

This book is about orienting life and ministry around desire—not the scandalous kind of desire, but the good kind, the *best* kind, where teenagers actually want to follow in the way of Jesus and participate in the kingdom. These are the desires that bring us into proximity with the One who imagined desire in the first place.

To be a youth pastor is to care about what teenagers want and to help them connect that desire with God. At our best, we cultivate adolescents' desire to follow in the way of Jesus—whatever that looks like for them—for the rest of their lives.

It's not earth-shattering, but I think it's a new way of approaching our work with students.

Whatever good you find in these pages, please keep. Whatever causes you shame or harm, please dismiss it—that is not my intention.

And if you're uncomfortable, please hang in there and know that you are not alone. I'm uncomfortable too.

2
WHO TOLD YOU THAT YOU WERE NAKED? OR, A THEOLOGY OF DESIRE

Is it not by his high superfluousness we know
Our God? For to equal a need
Is natural, animal, mineral: but to fling
Rainbows over the rain
And beauty above the moon, and secret rainbows
On the domes of deep sea-shells,
And make the necessary embrace of breeding
Beautiful also as fire,
Not even the weeds to multiply without blossom
Nor the birds without music:
There is the great humaneness at
the heart of all things,
The extravagant kindness, the fountain
Humanity can understand, and would flow likewise
If desire and power were perch-mates.

—Robinson Jeffers, "The Excesses of God"

Do you remember the last student you sat down and talked with? Maybe you've had trouble connecting with her. Maybe he's your favorite. Maybe she reminds you of yourself at that age. Picture that student's face. Imagine his or her voice, gestures, and facial expressions. Remember how he or she fidgets with their phone. Hear the student's laughter.

My student is Kenzie. She is beautiful, empathetic, ambitious, and as stubborn as they come. Kenzie loves adventure and sometimes mistakes it for harmful drama. She is one of the most honest young people I've ever met, and she has shown me more of who God is than I can say. Kenzie is so good.

Now we need to use our imaginations. As I'm talking with Kenzie, picture a shadow commandeering our conversation, stepping between the two of us and hiding Kenzie from my sight. Imagine that this presence is the very embodiment of sin and evil. (Try not to picture someone you know, tempting as that may be.)

I can no longer see Kenzie. Sin has taken her place at the table. She's lost; Kenzie has become sin.

Really? Of course not. If this happened, I would punch the evil thing in the throat and do everything I could to reveal the true Kenzie again.

Yet this is what common theology would lead us to believe about the brokenness of the world. We've believed that evil—sin, Satan, the devil, whatever you want to call it—has the power to define us and change our being. It has usurped our goodness.

Our theology has allowed sin to take control of our being. Honestly, I'm not comfortable giving evil that much power. It doesn't have the authority to become or define Kenzie. Or you.

Or me.

My job is to find Kenzie, not convert the sin. Yet the church has insisted that we become converters of sin, rather than seekers and finders of the real Kenzie.

I don't think this is how it's supposed to be. Don't get me wrong, I'm not naïve enough to deny sin and suggest that we are a flawless cast of *My Little Ponies* living in a utopian dreamland. This world is broken, full of instances and systems of evil; and sometimes my action or inaction contributes to that brokenness. If we're honest, we can feel the groaning of creation in our bones. We are no strangers to evil.

So I get why widely accepted Christian theology tells us we are depraved. Sinners. Dust. The scum of the earth. Inherently fallen. Worldly. Dirty. This message helps us make sense of how the world got to be so messed up.

I'm just not sure it's the original story. We've had to change it to soothe our confusion, fears, and doubts. Our usual narrative goes something like this:

> In the beginning, God created everything and called it good. God made human beings to look something like God. But then a serpent tempted them to be like God, and everything went rather badly. That badness thus defined humanity, and the whole world was evil. But then it was all okay again because Jesus came to earth to suffer, die, and forgive our sins. So if we accept Jesus into our hearts, we'll be forgiven for being so constantly, inherently bad.

> We'll be saved, but there's a sinking feeling that if we don't believe just right or have our 15-minute devotional in the morning, then all of that saving might wear off.

So have faith! And then one day after you die, you'll get to go to heaven where everything will finally be okay.

Somehow we think this is good news. It's not awful, but it's not good either.

We've taught teenagers that their wiring is inherently, unavoidably corrupt. It's no wonder teenagers feel compelled to constantly rededicate their lives to Jesus. After all, if you're made of dirt, then you can never be sure that you're really clean. From a young age, our students have been taught that they're bad, and then they're asked to believe that God loves them no matter what—except God will send them to hell if they don't love God back.

This is the gospel we offer: God loves you unconditionally; but if you don't love God back, then you're going to hell forever.

The church has passed its faith along perfectly and quite clearly, and we have been found wanting.

In my current job, I get to be a youth pastor, and I'm also trying my hand at children's ministry for the first time. I'm learning many things, but the thing that stands out the most is how anxiety about salvation gets rooted in our children early on.

We are so committed to the idea of original sin that it seeps into our second graders.

One day I was talking with the young elementary school kids about how God loves everyone, and this second grade boy named Alex looked at me defiantly and said:

Alex: "God doesn't love me!"
Me (*looking like a kicked puppy*): "Alex, there are a lot of things I don't know, but I am totally, 100 percent

convinced that God loves you."

Alex: "No way. I'm a total jerk. There's no way God could love a total jerk like me."

Me: "You know what, Alex? I don't think you're a jerk at all. And you know what else? God even loves total jerks."

Alex: "God would have to be really weird to love total jerks."

Me: "Then I think God's really weird *and* God loves you a lot."

The question that screams in my head is the same one that God asked Eve and Adam right after the fall: "Who told you that you were naked?!" Alex, who said you are a total jerk? Who told you that you are unlovable?

No wonder our teenagers will do anything to feel accepted, loved, desired, important, and beautiful. Our "good news" has denied it to them since they were kids. The first thing they're taught to internalize about God is that they're sinful, so we set them up to believe God can't possibly like the same things they like. Their desires must also be inherently bad—something to be conquered and silenced so they can want what God wants, even though they're not sure what that is.

I've always been confused about this message because that's not how the story begins. In the beginning there was:

Goodness.

Over and over and over God calls creation good.

Light. Sky. Sun. Moon. Stars. Oceans. Land. Plants. Birds. Fish. Animals. People. Rest.

Good.

So much good.

A world saturated and drenched with goodness.

And there are two good people who live in this natural wonder called Eden. Eve and Adam walk with God; they are naked but not ashamed.

We all know this beautiful place, this heaven on earth, gets broken. It has something to do with a serpent, a mysterious tree, and some oddly powerful fruit.

This moment somehow convinced the church that all is lost. The way we read Genesis 3 has us believing that we are marked and plagued by original sin, striving in vain to regain our goodness.

Really? What if that's not how we have to read it?
What if we keep reading the story of creation as something that's still dripping with goodness and desire—even after it's broken?

> In the beginning when God created the heavens and the earth, the earth was a formless void and darkness covered the face of the deep, while a wind from God swept over the face of the waters. (Genesis 1:1–2)

For six days God created, and God saw all that was being made and called it good.

I love to imagine the afternoon of the sixth day. I think the ancient authors of Genesis did too, since they told it twice (Genesis 1 and 2). They couldn't do it justice with only one go.

Each account is different and offers the creation of humanity from a unique perspective, like different camera angles on the same scene. The ancient rabbis used to say: Hold up Scripture to the light like a multifaceted jewel, and see the multitude of meanings it can hold. (I think this is why we all have so many opinions!)

The first angle, in Genesis 1, captures this mysterious triune God's desire: "God said, 'Let us make humankind in our image [*tselem*], according to our likeness [*demut*] . . . '" (1:26). "So God created humankind in [God's] image, in the image of God [God] created them; male and female [God] created them" (1:27).

In the beginning was desire. God wanted people. There's no other reason for doing all of this creating, is there? God wasn't lonely or bored or needy. God *wanted* us.

In Hebrew the words for "image" (*tselem*) and "likeness" (*demut*) are different. "Image" carries a much more tangible sense of similarity. *Tselem* is about a statue or a physical embodiment. In the ancient Near East, at the time when Genesis was written, this word would be used for the belief that a king was the physical body or presence of his god on earth— the incarnation, if you will.

On the other hand, "likeness," or *demut*, suggests a more abstract sort of representation. *Demut* was about similarity of characteristic, the way a daughter might learn to emulate her mother's gestures, expressions, and desires.

The second angle, in Genesis 2, zooms in for a closer look at the beautiful intimacy between God and humanity at the moment of creation. "Then the LORD God formed man from the dust of the ground, and breathed into his nostrils the breath of life; and the man became a living being" (2:7).

You have to really, really like someone to blow into her nose. Or it needs to be a matter of life and death. Maybe it was both. I think the most amazing part of creation is that it didn't have to happen. God was existing just fine—Father, Son, and Holy Spirit were hanging out, and they *wanted* to create. They had this desire to share love and community beyond themselves. Maybe it's a little like two people who are so in love that they desire to bring a new life into the world, a plant or a puppy or a baby, to share in all the goodness.

These scenes are where the idea of the *Imago Dei* comes from, that human beings are set apart from the rest of creation because we look something like God. We embody God's presence; we resemble God in some way.

There are a hundred ways of explaining how human beings look like God. For centuries theologians have wrestled with how to explain the *Imago Dei*, and they've come up with all sorts of ideas—facets on the jewel, if you will. We are like God because we have free will, we have the capacity to be like God, we are able to show the world what our God is like, we are able to love.

I'd like to add another: Because we are made in God's image, we desire.

What if we're made in the image of the One Who Desires? I wonder if this is what sets humanity apart from everything else and makes us the image and likeness of God: In all of creation, people have the capacity to desire—to want more—to actively hope.

Other created beings certainly have objectives that allow them to survive—everything has to eat. But desire takes humans *beyond* basic necessity. In all of creation, people have a unique capacity for wanting much more than we need. It's not a necessity for survival or an advantage to help us navigate natural selection. Humanity is like God because we have the ability, in our goodness, to desire.

As much as I love to ascribe human qualities to my golden retriever, Toby, he is and always will be motivated by his instincts. His necessities are food, water, shelter, and—I think I'd also argue—affection. On a regular basis, I'm able to convince myself that he is looking at me in adoration, rather than trying to Jedi mind-trick me into giving him snacks. Toby does not have thoughts of self-actualization. He does not dream of the dog he could be if he had a different collar or stopped sleeping so much or finally barked up that cute girl dog down the street.

Humanity's ability to desire is what makes temptation work so well. Before the fall, people walked with God, naked and unashamed. Made in God's image, they were secure in their identity as God's children. Then this serpent came along and what was the temptation? To eat fruit from this particular tree. They weren't hungry for food. They didn't need sustenance—they could eat anything and everything else in the garden. Yet if they ate from this tree . . .

They'd be like God, having knowledge of good and evil.

But they already *were* like God. They were made in God's image, created in God's likeness. They probably could have confirmed this with God face to face, had any doubts crept in.

Yet they wanted *more*.

They had this good desire to look more like this God they loved so much. It's just like when Peter wanted to walk on water and be like Jesus . . . but that comes later.

Temptation works best when it makes us doubt who we are.

Perhaps Eve and Adam thought, *Maybe we aren't enough like God? Maybe the fruit will help us be more like the man and woman God created us to be? Maybe . . . ?*

So they took a bite, wanting to make sure they really were who God said they were. And the world began to crack and break.

The origin of all sin is doubting that we are made in the image of God, and not trusting that we are good enough just the way we are. All sin is a distortion of good desire.

Three clues tell us the world will never be the same: Eve and Adam realized they were naked. They were ashamed. And they hid.

Honestly, I think if all of humanity suddenly became inherently sinful, then the writers of Genesis would have made a point of telling us about it. Or God would have been much angrier. Instead, we get a picture of heartbreak, where shame replaces trust and hiding replaces intimacy.

I imagine God's eyes brimming with tears: "Where are you? Who told you that you were naked? Sweet girl, dear boy, don't you know I love you? Who told you to hide? Who made you doubt that you are good like me? Who twisted your good desire?"

Humanity broke God's heart by not believing we were good enough. It wasn't a matter of wanting something different or something evil, it wasn't a matter of wanting to become our own gods. The problem is we doubted that we were already made in the image of God.

It's important to know that Eden probably didn't immediately look like Gotham City. It took time for the world to get dark. The sneaking suspicion that we are not enough was all it took for evil to enter the world. And the not-enoughs just piled up. We know what that's like.

It's easy to forget you look like God when you haven't seen God in a while.

We can imagine Cain was frustrated by his farm work and felt like God didn't think he was as good as his brother Abel. Cain just wanted to please God.

We can imagine Jacob feared that as the second-born son he didn't matter to his father, so he tricked his brother Esau and his father into giving him the firstborn's blessing. Jacob just wanted to be blessed.

We can imagine King Saul felt insecure about his military leadership when young David slew Goliath on the first try, so he tried to have David killed a few times. Saul just wanted the people's respect.

We can imagine Solomon wanted his father's approval and thought he could be good enough if he acquired a lot of wealth and built the temple that David never did. Solomon just wanted to be known for who he was, not for who his father was.

We can imagine. All the brokenness in the world comes from not believing there is enough goodness to go around.

That doesn't mean our deep desires are excuses for doing horrible things. The human condition isn't that we are evil; it's that we are terrified—either we fear we aren't good enough, or we fear there will never be enough goodness for us. Basically, it's like a game of musical chairs, except we're playing with a whole world full of people who'll do anything to have a chair.

Because God didn't create us to just stand there feeling all insecure and awkward once the music stops.

This is why we have favorite Bible verses. It doesn't matter if we have to take them completely out of context or borrow them from the people they were originally intended for. If it speaks to our desires, it belongs to us and applies to our lives. Grab it before it's gone. Make sure you claim it before the music stops.

The Christian practice of having a "life verse" is really about finding a part of Scripture that speaks to our desires and our deep fear that we aren't worthy of what we want. (Except for those folks who can't stand to pick a "popular" verse, so they go out of their way to choose a verse like Acts 10:13—"Then a voice told him, 'Get up, Peter. Kill and eat.'"—which still speaks to their desire to be unique and hilarious.)

The world denies our good desires all the time.
Not to worry.
There's a verse for that.

Want to be reminded that God loves you?
"For God so loved the world that [God] gave [God's] only Son, so that everyone who believes in him may not perish but may have eternal life" (John 3:16).

Want reassurance about paying back those student loans?
"For surely I know the plans I have for you, says the Lord, plans for your welfare and not for harm, plans to give you a future with hope" (Jeremiah 29:11).

Want to know that everything happens for a reason?
"We know that all things work together for good for those who love God, who are called according to [God's] purpose" (Romans 8:28).

Want God to be your life coach?

"I can do all things through [God] who strengthens me" (Philippians 4:13).

Want to stop staring at a screen and go for a hike?

"[Jesus said,] 'I came that they may have life, and have it abundantly'" (John 10:10b).

Even sarcasm reveals that we want good things.

We desire love.

We desire hope.

We want to know that everything will be okay.

Everything boils down to good humans wanting good things.

Have you ever experienced a moment when everything was exactly the way it was meant to be?

Playing with a puppy.

Talking with a soul mate.

Eating a ripe peach right off the tree.

Driving at twilight on a summer evening with the windows down and the perfect song playing on the radio.

Singing along to your favorite band with a thousand strangers.

Someone loves you even when you feel you don't deserve it.

Embracing a community of people who embraces you too.

And reconciliation of any kind.

This is what the kingdom of heaven is all about. The kingdom is any place where good desires reign supreme, where things are the way they're meant to be. We talk about it as God's presence, or heaven on earth, or wow.

All Jesus talked about was the kingdom of God. It was scandalous to proclaim good news to everyone when it's obvious that our broken world doesn't have enough good to go around.

At the beginning of his ministry, Jesus was invited to preach in his hometown. His family was probably there, along with his former neighbors and childhood friends. The synagogue was hushed with anticipation as Jesus stood and unrolled the scroll of the prophet Isaiah. Of all the texts he could have chosen, his finger traced the letters until he found the place where it was written:

> "The Spirit of the Lord is upon me,
> because he has anointed me
> to bring good news to the poor.
> He has sent me to proclaim release to the captives
> and recovery of sight to the blind,
> to let the oppressed go free,
> to proclaim the year of the Lord's favor."
> (Luke 4:18–19; cf. Isaiah 61:1–2)

No one moved. All eyes were locked on Jesus as he rolled up the scroll and sat down.

Then Jesus said, "Today this scripture has been fulfilled in your hearing" (4:21).

This was the framework for Jesus' whole ministry. We can imagine that he asked himself over and over again, *What is good news for this person right now?*

This is the best question ever. Want to understand what Jesus is up to? Think about who he interacted with, imagine what good news might be to that person, and then watch how Jesus responded.

This is, after all, where we get the word *gospel*. It means "good news." If you're talking with somebody about the gospel and she doesn't seem to be getting it, then it probably isn't registering as good news to her. Sight for the blind is part of the gospel, but that's not very helpful to someone who's deaf.

Jesus responded to people particularly, specifically, and exactly where they were at. He took the time to see them, to understand the good desires that ran beneath the surface of their outward situation, and then he offered them a taste of heaven.

Sometimes it's painfully straightforward. Sick people want to be well. Blind people want to see. Hungry people want something to eat. Mourning people want their loved ones to live again.

Sometimes it takes a little more patience and understanding to see where things are broken. Jesus knew that emotional and spiritual healing are just as important as physical healing.

In Jesus' day, lepers were exiled from their whole community. They literally became untouchable. In order to walk through a populated area, they had to warn people away by smashing wooden blocks together and yelling, "UNCLEAN! UNCLEAN!"

So when Jesus met a leper, he'd touch the person before he healed him (Luke 5:12–16). It's good news to be touchable, to be welcomed back to human contact. It's also good when your toes don't fall off. They're both good.

A woman caught in the act of adultery was brought before Jesus and a bunch of religious leaders. The Pharisees and scribes were testing Jesus because Moses' law called for this woman to face the death penalty. We can imagine she was terrified, humiliated, half-clothed or even naked before the judging stares of all these (self-)righteous men. Jesus' first impulse was to bend down and write in the dirt, which immediately drew everyone's eyes away from the woman. She was not condemned by Jesus or anyone else (John 8:2–11). It is good news to be treated with dignity and to be given life instead of death. They're both good.

Zacchaeus was a tax collector and he was short. The Israelites would have viewed him as a traitor, a puppet of the Roman empire, a sellout, and a cheater who charged more than he should and kept the extra as a personal bonus. He was an outsider among his own people. Zacchaeus desperately wanted to see who Jesus was, so he climbed a tree because he couldn't see over the crowd. Not only did Jesus notice him, but he invited himself over for dinner and then reminded Zacchaeus that he is a son of Abraham. He belonged with the people of Israel (Luke 19:1–10). It's good news to be seen, to be told that you belong, and to eat with Jesus.

Jesus' whole ministry can be seen through the lens of this question: What is good news here? To her? To him? To them?

When Jesus said, "The kingdom of heaven has come near" (Matthew 4:17), he didn't mean everything was going to be all right immediately or forever. Even the folks he healed got sick again. The folks he fed got hungry again. We can assume that eventually Lazarus died, again.

"The kingdom of heaven has come near" is an invitation to see that God is already at work restoring the world, even though it's not completely finished yet. The world is full of brokenness, and evil is a problem. It's just not *our* problem in the sense that we are evil. We're good. Yet over the course of human history, the original doubt, shame, and insecurity of the fall have made human civilization suspicious of goodness. We can never tell if there will be enough good to go around, we fear we will be taken advantage of, we want more and more and more. This deep-seated suspicion is what broke us and created worldwide systems of injustice—not the misplaced idea that humans are evil.

As we become people who are attuned to the goodness of humanity and the holiness of desire, we are invited to join God in bringing heaven to earth.

To follow in the way of Jesus is to follow in the way of desire. The gospel, the good news, calls to each person's God-given goodness and asks: What do you want?

3
TO DESIRE IS HUMAN

When we speak about holy things, I believe we have to write our thoughts in pencil, open to the possibility that the living God will take us by surprise and show us something new.

I have a theory (written in pencil) about how people relate to God. It seems to me that different sorts of people are drawn to God in different ways, and this makes me wonder how wise it is to have one God who is also three. We play favorites among the Trinity, which is a normal thing to do with complex relationships.

Many people are on Team Creator God. These people of faith believe God has been at work from the beginning of time to restore all things. Sometimes they are drawn to the power of the Almighty, the comfort of the Father, the ever-presence of the Alpha and Omega. They act as our priests who hold the faith, interceding with God on behalf of the world.

Some people are on Team Holy Spirit. These are the hopeful ones, the rebels, the creatives who believe the Spirit saturates the world with God's presence and creativity. They are enchanted with mystery. They are the prophets who look for truth and speak it boldly, inviting the world to wake up to thin places where heaven meets earth.

Other people are on Team Jesus. These are the lovers, the servants, the real-time ambassadors of the kingdom. They believe Jesus came to remind humanity what we were made for, to show us how God would live as a person in a specific place and time. These are the kings and queens who live to see the gospel become reality.

Which team is right? Which is wrong? Would any of us wish for their favorite person of the Trinity to stage a coup? Of course not. We are drawn to the multiplicity of God because we are sure of God's unity. Everyone is invited into relationship with the triune God. Relationships are dynamic and occasionally messy, and sometimes we play favorites. We are all members of one body, remember?

For all of our systematic theology and multistep discipleship models, the Christian faith is rooted in paradox. We believe all sorts of things that don't make sense when you look at them from a linear, logical standpoint:

God is one, and God is Father, Son, and Holy Spirit.
The kingdom of God is already here, and it's not here yet.
Lose your life and you will find it.
The weak are strong.
The first are last, and the last are first.
Jesus is fully human and fully God.

The ancient Hebrews called this concept "block logic." It's much different than the step logic we tend to prefer, where an argument progresses in a coherent, rational way. Block logic is a way of thinking that can hold many different concepts as truth, even if they seem to contradict each other.

Instead of either/or, block logic is all about the yes/and. It all depends on your perspective or context.

People are made in the image of God.
God is good, yes. And people are good.
God's desires are good, yes. And people's desires are good.
To be human is to desire, and desire is good.

A desire is something we want that we suspect would make us more whole. More alive. More ourselves. To be whole is to live into who we were uniquely created to be. To be whole is the goal of being a person.

God's ultimate desire for humanity is that we be completely ourselves, so we can most fully show our neighbors what God is like. We are made to reflect God's complete mercy by our mercy, God's complete justice by our work for justice, God's complete love by our generous love. Our desires lead us to reflect more and more who God is.

Even when we're doing things we don't particularly want to do, we are likely working toward something we want more, or more urgently.

If we're going to have an honest conversation about desire, we have to talk about both its beauty and its brokenness. We live in a world that's messed up, a world that bears the weight of individuals and systems who have forgotten they are good.

We are made in the image of the One Who Desires, but we're not perfect. As imperfect people, there are perfect and not-yet-perfect ways that desire plays out in our lives. We experience ways of being that are good and moments of being that are not-yet-good.

Yes. And. Desire hurts us. And people can be terrible. And people can want terrible things. Desire is so complex. The church has valid reasons for viewing "the world" or "the flesh" as the root of all sin and evil. Our good desires can manifest themselves in dark and twisty ways, but that doesn't mean we are evil or that our desires are always sinful. We look for fulfillment in all kinds of ways that don't satisfy us.

We know how this works. We've seen it over and over again in our kids.

A student starts doing drugs.
Is she doing drugs just because that is her heart's desire?
Not likely. Teenagers are complex humans, and this sort of disordered desire could mean she is turning to drugs to get what she wants—community, relaxation, attention, pleasure—thinking it will satisfy her.
There is always a story behind brokenness.
All sin is a distortion of good desire.

Honoring our desires means acknowledging that everything is not as it should be. Something is lacking. Somehow the world is broken. Every Christian theory about desire must be honest about the reality of evil in the world. If we listen to our desires, they will tune us in to the heartbreak of creation, the part that moans with grief and longs for restoration.

Sometimes we live too long in the land of not-yet-perfect, and coming back to our good selves becomes a painful, difficult process. Maybe this is what we mean by God's discipline, God's justice—it's meant to bring us back to ourselves when we've forgotten to be good.

C. S. Lewis had a brilliant imagination for this process. In *The Voyage of the Dawn Treader*, Eustace Scrubb is a miserable young boy who, we can only assume, has lived away from his own goodness for so long that no one can stand him. He becomes a dragon on an enchanted island, and no one can figure out how to change him back. Just when he has given up all hope, Aslan the Lion appears and tells Eustace he will feel better if he undresses and submerges himself in a pool of water. As dragons don't wear clothes, this means Eustace must shed his reptilian skin.

He tries and tries, but he can't get the scales to come off. So Aslan offers his assistance. Eustace tells the story like this:

> "The very first tear he made was so deep that I thought it had gone right into my heart. And when he began pulling the skin off, it hurt worse than anything I've ever felt. The only thing that made me able to bear it was just the pleasure of feeling the stuff peel off. You know—if you've ever picked the scab of a sore place. It hurts like billy-oh but it *is* such fun to see it coming away. . . ."

> "Well, he peeled the beastly stuff right off—just as I thought I'd done it myself the other three times, only they hadn't hurt—and there it was lying on the grass: only ever so much thicker, and darker, and more knobbly-looking than the others had been. And there I was as smooth and soft as a peeled switch and smaller than I had been. Then he caught hold of me—I didn't like that much for I was very tender underneath now that I'd no skin on—and threw me into the water. It smarted like anything but only for a moment. After that it became perfectly delicious and as soon as I started swimming and splashing I found that all the pain had gone from my arm. And then I saw why. I'd turned into a boy again."[4]

It's really difficult to hold the tension between our glory and our sins. It's hard to be a dragon when you know there's a human inside. It's much, much easier to say that one thing is right and the other is wrong, that one group is in and the other is out. If humans are evil, it makes sense that the world is messed up. Then we know where we stand. It's easier, but it's not good news.

Good news is a moving target. It depends on who, and when, and where you are. Jesus responded to people with the good news of the moment and the promise that one day there would be good news for *all* moments.

This is why Christians are a confessing people. We know everything is not the way it's supposed to be, and we know we play a role. We can be so far removed from the true goodness we possess. In my Episcopal tradition, we:

> "Confess that we have sinned against [God] in thought, word, and deed, by what we have done, and by what we have left undone. We have not loved [God] with our whole heart; we have not loved our neighbors as ourselves . . . ."[5]

We are all doing the best we know how. Desire is complicated.

We know we don't always want what is good. For instance, I know Dr. Pepper is a terrible choice for my health. I do not desire the negative consequences of pumping that much sugar, caffeine, and chemicals into my body on a regular basis. I know I'd feel better if I stopped drinking it. But it tastes like carbonated unicorn laughter, and I want it so much. I am writing this book at a time when my desire to live more healthily is as strong as it's ever been. I am meditating on humanity's good desires day and night, yet I find it nearly impossible to write without artificial stimulation of some sort.

I don't like coffee. Wine makes me sleepy. So this book is brought to you by Dr. Pepper and Starbuck's Grande-Two-Pump-Vanilla-Nonfat-No-Water-Chai-Lattes. That's not what I want, but I want to write this book more.

The apostle Paul is usually pretty articulate, but his desires baffled him:

> I do not understand my own actions. For I do not do what I want, but I do the very thing I hate. Now if I do what I do not want, I agree that the law is good. But in fact it is no longer I that do it, but sin that dwells within me. For I know that nothing good dwells within me, that is, in my flesh. I can will what is right, but I cannot do it. For I do not do the good I want, but the evil I do not want is what I do. Now if I do what I do not want, it is no longer I that do it, but sin that dwells within me. (Romans 7:15–20)

If Paul shared the conventional wisdom that humanity is inherently sinful, I don't think he'd be quite so conflicted. If he already believed he was evil, then why put up such a fight? This would read more like, "I know exactly what's going on here. I was created bad, and so I do bad things—even though my faith in Jesus makes me wish I were good. Bummer."

Instead, Paul is reflecting what we all experience—the disparity between our good selves and how frustrating it is that sometimes we choose death instead of life.

Wrestling with desire means embracing this paradox: Human desire is good, and humans don't always do good. If humans want good things, how come there is so much tragedy in the world? Two things that seem to conflict can be true at the same time.

Whether what we want brings us closer to life or closer to death, it shapes who we are and how we live. Our desires are fundamental to our personhood. There are different types of desire—some more superficial than others—and we'll talk about how those impact the way we live. Sometimes obstacles stand in the way of achieving our desires, and those are part of our formation too.

Two different categories of longing are almost always connected: craving and desire. One has to do with immediate gratification, the other with love. One is about satisfying the appetite of the moment; the other is about satisfaction, happiness, and joy that have longevity. The first can be either good or broken; the second is almost always good.

As a rule of thumb, people want good things. We are, after all, made in the image of the God who is both good and desiring. We all have different priorities; and sometimes things get dark and twisty when it comes to getting what we want, because we were hurt or we had a bad experience that confused goodness with badness.

What we crave is often the outward manifestation of a deeper good desire. We want all sorts of things so we'll feel safe, or loved, or meaningful, or wanted.

We are shaped most profoundly by moments where someone is able to read between the lines and see our true desires beneath our cravings. Have you ever experienced a moment when someone truly saw you, cutting through whatever was happening on the surface and taking a risk to name the desire she saw in you? These people are like Jacob, waking up and pointing out the reality of God's presence where we least expected it (Genesis 28:10–19).

My professor for my first seminary class was Jacob to me. The first session of the course was uneventful until the very end when he got a little misty-eyed. He looked at us; I mean, he really took his time to look around the room and meet all of our eyes. And in the sincerest voice you can imagine, his voice cracked a little with emotion as he said: "I am honored to learn with you this term. Thank you for being here. Each of you reveals God to the world in a way that no one else ever has, or can, or will . . . and I can't wait to get to know you."

Naming desire is to walk on holy ground. Desire is where we take off our shoes and expect to encounter God. To get to that point is often an adventure in paying attention and looking for where God already is in the midst of goodness, love, beauty, truth, and life.

Consider a middle school girl—we'll call her Beth—who is painfully aware that her peers all seem to have the newest cell phone. It's bigger, faster, clearer, and way more awesome than the clunky old flip phone her dad gave to her when his work issued him a new phone. Her family is middle class. With the recent state of the economy, it's been hard for her parents to make ends meet even though they both work hard at their respective jobs.

At the dinner table one night, Beth puts forth the request she's been rehearsing in her head all day: "Mom, Dad, can I get a new phone?" Beth goes on, in an increasingly desperate tone, to sing the praises of the particular device she has in mind. Oh, and everyone at school already has one! So there.

Beth's parents listen intently, trying to honor this thing their daughter craves. They explain, as gently as they can, that it's not something the family can afford right now. If she'd like to save up for it and chip in some money for the extra data fees each month, then she is welcome to make the upgrade. The dining room explodes.

Night after night for the next week, Beth and her parents go around and around the issue, their voices rising higher each time they discuss it. Mom and Dad are shocked that their good daughter would respond so outrageously over a silly phone. Especially when she already has a cell phone that works just fine!

The argument seems ridiculous to both sides. Beth can't understand why her parents don't get that she needs a new phone. Beth's parents don't understand why Beth can't cope with using her old phone until she saves up enough money for a new one.

What's going on here? It's just a normal snapshot of an explosive, unpredictable, and entitled teenager, right?

This scene is all about the tension between the things we crave and the things we desire. What does desire have to do with craving a new cell phone? One of the clues that desire is at play in something we're craving is that we may be really attached to the idea and emotional about getting it.

Beth doesn't want a new, fancy phone just for the sake of having a new phone. For her, the phone is a step toward satisfying her desire to belong and feel connected to her community. If her current phone is something that other kids tease her about, she might feel embarrassed and self-conscious, and these feelings may trigger other areas of vulnerability for her. If people think that way about her phone, what must they think about her haircut? She feels left out when her friends are interacting via social applications, taking photos, and sharing their lives online. Beth is desperate not to be left behind.

The desires behind her craving are good desires—they're at the core of what it means to be human. But these desires were manifested in her craving for the new phone.

Some of the most sacred work we do with students is seeing what's going on beneath the surface. Cultivating adolescents' desire means we must learn to read their longings and their wounds beneath their external cravings.

Everything we do has a good desire behind it, even if the way we express that desire is broken or misguided. Therapists call this the "presenting problem." What is the external evidence of the inward process that's really the point of the whole thing? The presenting problem is rarely the fundamental issue or core desire; it's a symptom.

Sometimes good desires are veiled by fear or shame.

We all have tragedies that shape who we are: eating disorders, bullying, substance abuse, self-harm, compulsive overachievement. These experiences never stand alone. This is why we need counselors in the world—to help us see where the goodness of our desire was silenced, wounded, or denied. We'll never know until we ask our students to tell their stories. But if we begin from a place of trusting that these precious humans don't actually want harmful, disordered patterns in their lives, then it's easier to offer them love instead of condemnation.

To see that a student who dates compulsively is actually lonely is to name that he desires human connection and community—and this is good.

To see that a student who's involved in every extracurricular imaginable is actually terrified of being invisible or irrelevant is to name her good desire for significance.

To see that a student who's obsessed with video games and computers might have some social anxiety or wish to numb some internal pain is to name his good desire to feel connected and safe.

To see that a student who's preoccupied with her appearance might have low self-esteem is to name her good desire to be accepted for who she is.

I want to be careful not to oversimplify here. Many students are dealing with things that are quite serious, and we may not be qualified to help them process the desires behind them. Students who've been abused, who are suffering from substance addiction, and who struggle with serious emotional or physical issues need to be connected to a qualified professional. But how many of these significant issues go unseen because we're too busy paying attention to students' outward cravings and behavior, rather than trying to catch a glimpse of their underlying desires?

This is what it means to do life with and love our students. To know them well enough and care enough about them to see beyond what they portray to the world, asking them to speak to their inner reality where good desire resides.

Following our desires is the stuff of life.

Our experiences of desire, whether or not we achieve them, shape who we are. And these desires don't have to be specifically labeled "Christian" in order to be good news. Most of the time, they're not.

Think about the things that have most profoundly shaped you. Are they all specifically Christian?

Horses saved me long before Jesus did. I was a perpetually lonely kid who struggled to sort through my parents' divorce, and I was afflicted with horse-craziness. Craziness, I tell you.

The only gifts I received for the first 14 years of my life were horse-related. Seriously. I have a bronzed horse lamp.

I begged my parents for horseback riding lessons, and they caved. My wide-eyed enthusiasm made me the awkward preteen shadow of my saintly riding instructor, Judy. I wanted to be just like her, and I fancied myself as her protégé. Her patience and kindness ought to be the stuff of legend.

My desires helped me become who I am. As a preteen, horses gave me a taste of what it felt like to be confident in my body, to belong to a community, to have a hero who believed in me. Every penny I earned or received went toward my horse fund with the hope that one day I might possess the animal of my dreams. I thought I might die if I couldn't have a horse.

Then I turned 16. Some horrible horse-dream-killing switch went off inside my adolescent brain, and I knew what I had to do. Clearly I'd been saving all this time for a car, not a silly horse! This self-betrayal was only redeemed by the fact that my savings bought me a gorgeous 1965 Ford Mustang, in teal.

Good news is a moving target. It changes and bends as we live our lives and become who we will be. The desires that were once fulfilled by horses are still a part of who I am.

There's a reason everyone remembers their first car. You've seen the gleam in your friend's eyes as she describes the rusted-out hand-me-down Saturn she drove in high school. Even our cars can shape who we become. That Mustang offered me freedom and autonomy that I hadn't even realized I craved, as well as a profound sense of ownership and responsibility toward this valuable thing that was mine to care for.

Wherever we find goodness, truth, beauty, love, or life— we find something of God's presence and the reality of the kingdom on earth as it is in heaven. Humans are naturally drawn to good news when it's truly good.

If students actually want to follow Jesus and participate in the work of the kingdom, then there isn't much that can stop them. We all know that once a teenager's heart is set on something, she won't be deterred very easily.

The opposite is also true: if teenagers don't want God, Jesus, the church, the kingdom, or youth group, then there isn't much we can do to make them. Desire can't be thrust upon someone.

This is why all the fairy godmothers and genies in the stories can't promise to make the beloved fall in love with the hero. All the wishful thinking in the world can't compel desire.

Desire has to be wooed.

My job as a youth pastor is to cultivate adolescents' desires to be formed in the way of Jesus. This means inviting students' desires—whatever they may be—into conversation with their faith.

A lot of the time it feels like church, youth group, and all the trappings of faith are in competition with the rest of teenagers' lives. Youth group OR soccer. Mission trip OR choir trip. Retreat OR Boy Scouts. Sunday morning service OR camping with friends.

If our posture of ministry is about finding ways to coerce students into faith, then we're competing with everything. I apologize for saying this, but in my experience, the other stuff is usually better.

I've had parents ask me to start a church soccer team. Seriously? You'd rather have a youth pastor who's never played soccer in her life coach a soccer team so it has the proper Christian label? No. Go and join a community team, get to know some neighbors, and everything will be better.

We could lament to parents that even if students have great attendance at everything the youth group does, we'll still see them only 100 hours out of the year. We could say that's about 1 percent of a student's life that's set aside for God. Then guilt and shame can get to work. How will they ever be good Christians now? No wonder they're having all the sex.

If our posture of ministry is about finding ways to cultivate adolescents' desire for God, then the whole world becomes a playground where we play hide-and-seek with God.

Except, this is a God who wants to be found,
who rejoices in being pursued,
and then turns to find us,
again and again and again.

It's not a competition with the rest of life, and it can be so good.

What if the next time a student chooses to go to soccer practice instead of youth group, we ask him what he loves about soccer, instead of guilting him or passive-aggressively noting how much we missed him?

Maybe it's the camaraderie of the team,
or maybe he loves moving his body and running fast,
or perhaps he feels most confident when he's out on the field,
or it could be that it's the one place where he gets his dad's undivided attention,
or maybe he's terrified he won't get into college without more extracurriculars,
or perhaps it's just plain fun.

Very rarely will a teenager say, "I hate Jesus and church, so I went to soccer instead."

What if our response was:

"No wonder you love being part of a team; God made you for community."

"I'm so glad you're able to feel good in your body; God made our bodies so good."

"You have every reason to be confident because you're a child of God. I'm so glad playing soccer reminds you of that."

"Relationships with parents can be so tough. I would totally play soccer if it meant feeling closer to my family. I'm sorry your dad seems so far away. I know he loves you even if he can't be around all the time."

"Any college worth going to doesn't want you to play soccer because you feel like you have to. Are there other things you'd really like to do instead, things you'd be proud to tell an admissions board about?"

"Yes! Soccer *is* fun! God loves it when we play."

The sum of our desires and our brokenness conspire to make us who we are. They form us not only in our faith, but in our whole lives. Identity formation is one of the main tasks of adolescence. What teenagers decide about their desires determines who they will become. If God is connected to their good desires, it might be easier to imagine doing life with God beyond high school.

We deny our own Lord's Prayer when we insist that all goodness, life, love, beauty, and truth is found only within church contexts. Jesus taught us to pray that God's will be done on earth as it is in heaven—not only in the *church* as it is in heaven. In fact, it often seems like there is more good news happening outside of the church than inside. We need to let our students find that good news and teach us more about it.

The question those of us in youth ministry need to be asking is, "How do we connect adolescents' desires with the goodness of God and the unfolding reality of the kingdom?"

We must come alongside students—both lost and found, in the flock or on the fringe—and find ways to connect their deepest desires to the God who is ever present in goodness, beauty, truth, and love.

The best part? If we seek to form students according to their desires and teach them that God is already present in the goodness of those desires, then they will always be able to find God somewhere. In college. In a foreign country. In a conversation with a Muslim friend. In their vocation. In their families. In tragedy. In the way they care for their neighbors.

Our students will always have good desires.

May we learn to be the ones who remind them that God thinks so too.

4
BECOMING A
PERSON INSTEAD OF A
CHRISTIAN

You do not have to be good.
You do not have to walk on your knees
for a hundred miles through the desert, repenting.
You only have to let the soft animal of your body
love what it loves.
Tell me about despair, yours, and I will tell you mine.
Meanwhile the world goes on.
Meanwhile the sun and the clear pebbles of the rain
are moving across the landscapes,
over the prairies and the deep trees,
the mountains and the rivers.
Meanwhile the wild geese, high in the clean blue air,
are heading home again.
Whoever you are, no matter how lonely,
the world offers itself to your imagination,
calls to you like the wild geese, harsh and exciting–
over and over announcing your place
in the family of things.

— Mary Oliver, "Wild Geese"

There is a group of young professionals in Seattle that organizes massive snowball and water balloon fights for charity. More Seattleites come out for these events on a Saturday afternoon than sit inside all of the city's churches on a Sunday morning. During the "Snow Day" event on January 12, 2013, they broke the Guinness World Record for the world's largest snowball fight when 5,834 people showed up to play in the snow that they trucked in from mountains an hour away. Through this and other similar epic events, they've raised more than $100,000 for wonderful children's charities like the Boys and Girls Club.

In the shadow of the Space Needle on August 17, 2013, more than 4,000 people showed up for their "Party Camp" event, navigating a sea of kiddie pools overflowing with 300,000 water balloons. It's not every day that pummeling your friends with water balloons is considered altruistic. And the joy emanating from Seattle City Center was felt all across town— on buses, in restaurants, on social media. The Party Camp organizers gave Seattlites something they didn't even know they wanted.

They made generosity a delight instead of an obligation— and it worked. They raised $55,000 so patients at the Seattle Children's Hospital could go to summer camp. And it will work every time because no matter what words we use to describe transcendence, we find God at the intersection of delight and desire. It's an easy Would You Rather? proposition.

Neither event was designated as Christian, and I highly doubt anyone came to Jesus while lobbing snowballs or water balloons at strangers. But it kind of looked like the kingdom. I wonder if it might serve as a modern-day parable: the kingdom of God is like a big water balloon fight where everyone gets together and supports a good cause with great delight.

The most revolutionary thing that youth pastors can do is expand others' expectations of God, the kingdom, and the gospel. If we do only one thing for the rest of our lives, may it be to throw wide open the definition of God's presence and what it means to be saved.

The focal point of most student ministries is converting teenagers to the Christian faith. Our relationships, curricula, programming, worship, retreats, lock-ins, and service projects have a glaring ulterior motive: that young people would become Christians, bring their families and friends to church, and help the church make *more* Christians. We feel a huge wave of relief and triumph when they raise their hands—or better yet, cry—after we deliver a compelling gospel message and invite them to pray the salvation prayer.

Phew! They're in. We did well. Tell the elder board we're winning.

If 60 percent of young people are running from church as soon as they graduate from high school, we should consider the possibility that conversion-oriented ministry is failing. We can't scare, shame, or argue young people into the kingdom of God.

This conversion mentality is often rooted in a message of shame, which is antithetical to the good news. We perpetuate an oppressive system of sin management when we do altar calls based on students admitting they are bad, but if they decide to love God, then they'll become good. The church's tendency has been to beat people into becoming Christians with guilt and shame.

This way of ministry has minimized and demonized the good desires of young people, driving them away from church and faith. This is why so many people speak about how they like

Jesus but can't stand the church. Most churches only have room for niceness, not desire. We can't control or predict desire; it's too chaotic—and yet we follow a God who creates beauty and order out of chaos.

The gospel calls for more desire, not less. We read Bible stories of how people ripped their way through the roofs of homes, climbed trees, pressed through massive crowds, and even walked on water to be in the presence of Jesus. They brought their deepest desires to Jesus' feet because it was a matter of life and death. Our tired gospel offers atonement, but we need to be raised from the dead.

We forget how little conversion has to do with faith formation. Jesus wasn't looking for converts; he was looking for disciples with the capacity to desire the kingdom of heaven. Jesus' disciples didn't follow him to become more religious; they followed him to become more human and more whole.

The calling of the first disciples is billed as this amazing example of the disciples' instant devotion to Jesus. I imagine them reacting like zombies: Jesus (who looks airbrushed and Swedish) calls them, and they turn to follow him with blank stares and arms raised, moaning something about catching humans instead of fish. It's creepy, actually.

I love Rob Bell's exegesis of this encounter. He talks about how in ancient Israel the position of rabbi held great dignity within the community. Back then young Jewish boys dreamed of becoming a rabbi like boys today dream of becoming firefighters or astronauts. They would learn all about the stories of God from these teachers, memorizing more and more of the first testament Scriptures during each year of their training. And then every year, the rabbi would invite some of the boys to continue their education, while sending the rest to go home and learn the family business. Only the best of the best students were invited to become disciples, and the rabbi would say to them, "Come, follow me."

This invitation didn't mean they could just tag along. Everyone knew what those words meant. If a rabbi invited you to follow him, he was saying: "I think you can be like me; I think you can do what I do." He chose very carefully because he knew one of these students would take his place as rabbi one day.

This bit of backstory entirely changes the scene. These men aren't mindless disciple puppets anymore. They are fishing, after all. At some point while they were growing up, a rabbi sent them home to learn their father's trade.

Jesus invited the disciples to remember their good desires, to resurrect childhood dreams that had been hushed by duty. Their hearts must have thrilled at his call to follow. *Me? You think I can be like you? You think I can do what you do? Have you heard the crazy stuff this guy does?*

No wonder they dropped their nets and followed Jesus. The fulfillment of good desire is irresistible.

In this story we hear Jesus repeat the miraculous promise that God made to humanity at creation: We can be like God.

Loving.
Good.
True.
Beautiful.
Alive.
Whole.

These are some of the words that the writers of Scripture offer to describe what God is like. Further, the author of Psalm 139 tells us the whole world is full of God's presence and there is nowhere we can go that God is not already there. This is the work of the Holy Spirit—to help us see that the world is saturated with holiness.

If God is love, then there is nothing God can do that is unloving. If God is love, then any love we encounter shows us something of what God is like. Any love. All love. Not just Christian love.

If Jesus is the way, the truth, and the life, then any truth or life we encounter must reveal something of Jesus' true way of life.

If God is just, then any instance of justice must reveal something of the way the world is meant to be when it is under God's reign.

God doesn't have a preferred brand of love, goodness, truth, beauty, life, or justice—God has a monopoly on these things. The gospel reminds us there is nothing proprietary about following God. Most of what belongs to God isn't labeled "Christian."

Let me be clear: This doesn't mean that everything good and beautiful and true is God, but it might reveal something of who God is, where God is, and what God is doing in the world. My dog is good and beautiful and full of life. He is not God, yet he reminds me of God every day.

We already do this! Whenever we come up with an illustration or an object lesson for our students, we're creating something holy from the mundane. Something will strike us and we'll talk about it because we think it might help them understand more about who God is. This is happening all the time, whether we name it and claim it as Christian or not.

After a brilliant meal, we'll say, "That was heavenly."
Or after visiting a particularly gorgeous place: "It was like
heaven on earth."
And the opposite is also true.
We see grievous injustice: "It's a living hell."
We know all too well where the kingdom of God is already and
where it's not yet.

This is what Jesus did all the time with his parables. We tend
to think of these stories as disembodied, just like our speaking
illustrations—life experiences that Jesus saved up for future
teachable moments. It's almost as if we believe he had a
pocketful of Post-Its with ideas scrawled across them. But
in reality, Matthew tells us Jesus didn't say anything to the
crowds without using a parable (Matthew 13:34–35). For Jesus,
every moment was teachable because the whole earth is full of
the presence of God.

We are drenched in holiness.

Jesus made eye contact with a farmer and his family. "A farmer
went out to sow his seed . . . " (Matthew 13:3, NIV). *Bam!*
Parable of the Sower.

He saw a mustard tree. "The kingdom of heaven is like a
mustard seed . . . " (Matthew 13:31, NIV).

He ate some bread for lunch. "The kingdom of heaven is like
yeast . . . " (Matthew 13:33, NIV).

He walked through the marketplace. "The kingdom of heaven
is like a merchant looking for fine pearls . . . " (Matthew 13:45,
NIV).

He smelled fishermen. "The kingdom of heaven is like a net
that was let down into the lake . . . " (Matthew 13:47, NIV).

Jesus' ministry was almost completely improvised because it depended on seeing God in the midst of life. He was predisposed to seeing glimpses of the kingdom everywhere he turned, and this was good news to everyone except those who thought they had a special claim to God's presence, goodness, truth, and love.

The best of humanity was found in Jesus because he rightly believed he was like God. Jesus did not come to earth so we would be Christians; Jesus came so we would be more human. The dream of the kingdom is that people will start believing they are good, that all good things are God's, and that they can participate in bringing more goodness to the world.

The best compliment I've ever received in youth ministry came from a dear friend after she began volunteering with our middle school students. She looked incredulous as she said, "You treat them like human beings!"

Offering dignity to teenagers' desires is kingdom work.

I would rather my students become whole humans than good Christians. This is the work of discipleship and spiritual formation. If we can help young people tune in to the goodness of their desires, I trust they will be drawn into the presence of God—whether they know it or not.

Do they love creating beauty? We say, "Keep pursuing beauty and you will find the One that all the beauty comes from."

Are they passionate for truth? We say, "Keep seeking truth, and you will find the Source of all truth."

Do they want to love and be loved? We say, "Keep loving, and you will know God, even if it's not by name."

This is the great coup of the kingdom: We can wake up and realize that God was all around us when we didn't even know it. We are created in the image of a desiring God so that all of our good desires woo us back to God.

Take another example from our patron saint of desire, C. S. Lewis. *The Last Battle*, the grand finale of The Chronicles of Narnia series, recounts the clash between those who follow the evil god, Tash, and those who follow the good Aslan. Emeth is a foreigner who has served Tash his whole life, but he finds himself miraculously invited into Aslan's country (heaven, presumably):

> "Lord, is it then true . . . that thou and Tash are one?"
>
> The Lion growled so that the earth shook . . . and said, "It is false. Not because he and I are one, but because we are opposites . . . For I and he are of such different kinds that no service which is vile can be done to me, and none which is not vile can be done to him. Therefore if any man swear by Tash and keep his oath for the oath's sake, it is by me that he has truly sworn, and it is I who reward him. And if any man do a cruelty in my name, then it is Tash whom he serves and by Tash his deed is accepted. Dost thou understand, Child?"
>
> I said, "Lord, thou knowest how much I understand . . . Yet I have been seeking Tash all my days."
>
> "Beloved," said the Glorious One, "unless thy desire had been for me thou wouldst not have sought so long and so truly. For all find what they truly seek."[6]

Everyone finds what they're looking for; we seek what we desire. We become what we desire. It forms us into a certain kind of person. Yet if we practice brokenness long enough, it's

83

hard to remember how to ask to be made whole again.

What if we became people who looked for the presence of God in everything good, true, beautiful, loving, and living? Spiritual formation and discipleship are about helping students tune in to their humanity and desires.

The gospel of shame and fear will never make us whole, for it denies that we are good—as if we've already surrendered to being something less than humans made in the image of God. Desire, on the other hand, is something we can live into, a way of being in the world that brings us into proximity with the living God and the unfolding reality of the kingdom.

If we can help students see God at work in whatever they desire that is good, true, beautiful, loving, and alive, then they will always be able to find and follow God.

For years now I've been orienting my student ministry around desire, but at first I was afraid I was breaking them. It can make for a weird youth group.

For instance, we have a strict code of honoring each other's desires. When we go places together in the van, they self-determine the music selection by taking turns: each student gets to play a song he or she likes, and no judgment is allowed. Top 40. Boy band. Screamo. Country. Techno. Classical. Repeat. I'm not kidding! These are normal kids who simply understand the goodness of their desires, and they respect the desires of others.

One Sunday, a student with Aspergers was having a particularly difficult time. My co-leader offered to take him out of the room to settle down and talk with him, but the group protested. They wanted to be with him, they said. They wanted to work it out together and understand what he wanted. This is what love looks like, they said.

No altar call does that. Trusting that we're good and tuning in to God's desires does that.

If we want to learn the gospel, we have to learn people. What are folks talking about in their neighborhood cafe? What are the top ten songs on iTunes? What's on the front page of Reddit? What books are sitting on the bestseller shelf at the local bookstore? What's everyone doing on Saturday?

Beyond superficial cravings, people want good, true, beautiful, lively, loving things.

If we believe those things reveal who God is, then our desires will always lead us into the presence of God.

Even the most broken wishes have good desires behind them. God doesn't look at the outward appearance—which is what we tend to look at. God looks at the heart. As we are formed in the way of Jesus, we become the sort of people who can see the good desires of even the most broken heart.

Let me be clear: This doesn't mean people are off the hook for acting out of misguided desire. Desire isn't a free pass that says whatever we crave at any given moment is good. Anyone who harms another person is not acting in the name of the One Who Desires, even if they claim it's what they want most. This is the definition of cheap grace: believing that just because God forgives or just because desire is good, we can do whatever we want and not be held accountable. Insisting that it's okay to desire hatred, fear, injustice, or violence is antithetical to the kingdom of God.

Repentance is about learning how to see through our own broken cravings and return to our God-given goodness.

Choosing life—following our good desires—is so costly.

Paul exhorts the Philippians to orient their lives around things which connect them to God:

> Finally, beloved, whatever is true, whatever is honorable, whatever is just, whatever is pure, whatever is pleasing, whatever is commendable, if there is any excellence and if there is anything worthy of praise, think about these things. (Philippians 4:8)

The people I respect the most are the ones who are more focused on becoming whole people, not specifically Christian people. I almost prefer it when I'm not sure a person even likes Jesus—like he or she is so consumed with living well that there is no time for labels. That person is pursuing the kingdom of God, whether or not he or she calls it that.

For instance:
Michelle Obama makes me want to work on my arms.
Rainn Wilson makes me want to ask better questions and never fear the answers.
Tina Fey makes me want to tell stories better.
Anne Lamott makes me want to be my messy self more fully.
Macklemore makes me want to make my work into an art form.
Mumford & Sons makes me want to create more heaven on earth.
My husband makes me want to be more like Jesus.

How does your youth ministry invite students to bring their desires to bear on their faith? How can what they care about most bring them into the presence of God? The ones who ask these questions are already close to the kingdom of heaven.

If we pay attention to desire, we run the risk of forming whole, healthy young people who are falling more and more in love with God and finding ways to participate in the restoration of all things. If they know there is room in God's kingdom for the things they care about most, it becomes much less likely that they'll look for salvation elsewhere.

The opposite is also true. If it seems as though the church has no room for what students believe is good, they will leave and find good news someplace else.

5
WIRED TO DESIRE

You'd think the church would be at the forefront of understanding human desire. The point of our programs, after all, is to cultivate desire and connect each other to the God who desires. We should be desire experts, naming and celebrating the good desires of the human heart while grieving the ways that desire becomes twisted.

What if we explored the ways that humanity is wired to reflect the One Who Desires?

Our colleagues in marketing, neuroscience, psychology, and sociology invest extravagantly in thousands of studies on adolescents each year. Advertisers spend a fortune exploring the connections between the latest scientific studies on adolescent development and how they can hone their marketing so it's most meaningful to teenagers. Companies enlist advertising firms and adolescent consultants in an effort to tap into adolescent desire. Why? Because it's estimated that young people spend $200 billion in discretionary income each year.

Desire is big business.

We'd do well to pay attention and borrow their groundbreaking insights for the sake of cultivating kingdom desire in adolescents.

When we talk about adolescent desire, the first thing we think about is sex. However, desire doesn't always refer to teenage hormones and sex. It turns out there is a lot more to desire than just raging hormones. We aren't forming students according to their hormones, but they should still be taken into consideration.

Adolescents are complex. Their task is to become a whole adult person; and their bodies, brains, hearts, and souls collaborate to make it happen. No part of them is at rest. They are strangers in a strange land, dealing with hair, hormones, emotions, and an ever-shifting social landscape.

For many, adolescence is the most glorified and glamorous season of human life. Children long to be adolescents, expressing their desire by emulating teenage styles, language, affinities, and actions. On the other end of the spectrum, adults often express a preference for the accouterments of youth culture, wishing to appear as young and trendy as their teenage children. The entertainment industry idolizes adolescence by casting 30-year-olds to play high school roles in movies and TV shows. They give teenagers a desirable yet developmentally impossible standard to meet, while offering hope to re-juveniled adults.

In many youth ministry books, an entire chapter is devoted to adolescent development because it's so important for youth workers to be able to begin where teenagers are at physically, emotionally, mentally, and socially. We've learned that:

> Teens are moving from the concrete thinking of childhood to the abstract thinking of adulthood—

as individuals, they'll be in unique places along that spectrum.

The infamous prefrontal cortex—the part of the brain that understands risk and foresees consequences— is still developing during adolescence, so teens may reflect that ongoing development with their risky or addictive behaviors.

Teens are flooded with emotions they don't always know how to deal with.

One of the primary tasks of adolescence is to differentiate from one's family and become more independent—this often looks like rebellious behavior.

Socially, teenagers are desperate to find belonging with peers who are also experiencing significant shifts in the tectonics of their bodies and brains.

Unfortunately, there has been little research in the realm of how teenagers form good desires. The prevailing research and rhetoric revolves around high-risk behavior, addiction, sexual practices, and marketability of brands.

Some people seem to understand the goodness of teenagers innately. Do you remember the teacher who helped you enjoy learning, or the coach who believed in you? We are shaped most profoundly by the people who tune in to our goodness and make us believe that our desires are worth pursuing.

Who helped make you into who you are today? What are their names?

Mr. Harper. His English class was the most formidable in all of middle school. He was also a master puppeteer. When he wasn't demanding that we learn the definitions and usage of a thousand master's-level vocabulary words, he was coaching us to put on puppet shows for sick children at local hospitals. It was serious, and it was awesome. Mr. Harper clearly believed we could be good at school and good at life, and he made it so we *wanted* to be. I still remember what *insipid* means, thanks to him.

Coach Wheeler, my high school softball coach. I was terrible; I literally spent my entire sophomore season learning rudimentary sports medicine and how to keep a stat book. Then during my senior year, Coach Wheeler invited me to be her assistant coach for the freshman softball team. Despite my mediocrity on the field, something made her believe that I could teach and encourage the younger girls. It was better news to me than if I'd started every game as a varsity player.

Coach Wheeler saw value in me to coach a game I couldn't play. I can look back and see how coaching those girls was part of my call to youth ministry. She believed in me and made me believe that I was good. And now I get to pass that gift along to my students.

Really good teachers, coaches, and youth pastors know how to cultivate desire.

If we pay attention to these cultivators, the latest research, and effective marketing strategies, there are compelling clues about how teenagers develop desire. Very intriguing patterns arise when we take a multidisciplinary approach to understanding the developmental processes behind why and how teenagers want good things.

The most common conversation in the world happens around 3 p.m., Monday through Friday.

Parent: "How are you?"
Teen: "Fine."
Parent: "What happened at school today?"
Teen: "Nothing."

Good talk.

Believe it or not, there are reasons why this parent-teen interaction is almost universal. So much is happening during this quick, eye-rolling dialogue. Adolescent brains are working overtime in a way that child and adult brains can't even imagine.

Some brain basics: We have three brains that work together as one.

Please don't use this as a new way to explain the Trinity, tempting as that may be. Our brains are not God; they're only God-like. If it helps, say *brains* like a zombie would every time you read it. BBBRRRAAAIIIIINNNSSSS.

The first brain is the brain stem, which controls your bodily systems. It allows you to breathe without having to think about it. You have no control here.

The second brain is the limbic brain, which is home to your emotions, hormones, and new information storage. You have very, very little control here.

The third brain, the cortex, helps you put words to everything. Your reason, intellect, and street smarts hang out here and try to make sense of all the signals coming from the limbic brain. You're in charge now.

The amygdala is responsible for your emotions. Basically, she's the drama queen, located right in the middle of everything.

She's more active during adolescence than at any other time of life. This tiny, sassy lump of brain triggers emotions based on the social information it receives from the frontal lobes, and it keeps a log of these reactions for future reference.

The temporal lobes are like your brain's therapist. They're responsible for interpreting and understanding emotion, and they're underdeveloped in adolescence (especially in guys). Emotions are difficult for teens to articulate because part of the frontal cortex produces spoken emotional language, and it's still under construction as well.

In his book *A Parent's Guide to Understanding Teenage Brains: Why They Act the Way They Do*, Mark Oestreicher gives a really helpful illustration for the emotional overdrive that is adolescence: Children are given a very basic palette of emotions to paint with. You've got your happy, sad, angry, and afraid. But when puberty kicks in, that drama queen amygdala becomes hyperactive and exchanges the basic palette for a *huge* spectrum of emotional options. Teens can be overwhelmed by the range of feelings they're experiencing, so they have a hard time processing, articulating, and regulating their responses.

Some students will embrace dramatic shifts between moods, painting a veritable rainbow of emotions during the course of a given day.

Others will respond by letting all the colors run together, creating a muddy taupe that seems easier to manage than having lots of distinct options.

It's understandable, then, that the emotions triggered by an innocent question such as: "How are you?" might be too daunting. It's easier for a teenager to just admit to being fine. I'm not sure parents would know what to do if their teenage daughter answered this question honestly:

"Well, this morning I was exhausted because I didn't get enough sleep, so I snapped at my little brother. I got kind of depressed while getting ready for school because I hate my elbows and my teeth aren't as white as Samantha's. I had to run to catch the bus, and I felt terrified that if I missed it, I'd have to beg for a ride or be late for my first-period English exam. I was totally relieved when I made it onto the bus though, and I was THRILLED when I saw Christy sitting on the bus because she'd been on vacation and I missed her so much and I LOVE her . . . "

And those are just the feelings she had by 8 a.m.

It's not just the plethora of emotions that overwhelms teenagers; it's figuring out how to interpret and communicate them. Their still-developing brains have trouble processing and regulating their emotional responses.

No wonder they say they're fine.

You wouldn't think asking what happened at school would be a loaded question, but for a teenager, it is.

The hippocampus lives right next door to the amygdala, and it stores all of the new information that comes into the brain. During adolescence the hippocampus is in overdrive, absorbing stimuli from all over the brain about what the teenager is seeing, hearing, tasting, touching, and smelling. Teenagers are literally built to be learning machines.

You'd think this stage of development would be an exciting and compelling time for young people. No doubt it is, at some point. We've all seen children—and even young teens—who are excited to go to school. But then out of nowhere, a switch gets flipped and school is worse than vegan corndogs. I'm sure that transition is complicated for teens, but at least part of it can be blamed on their brains.

Deep in our brains is the pleasure center, the nucleus accumbens. These are awesome because they receive dopamine, the hormone that triggers the endorphins that make us feel pleasure. Together they make a sort of reward system, because clearly we'd rather feel good than bad. Humans are hard-wired to make choices that make us feel good.

The number of receptors that the nucleus accumbens have for dopamine is highest during adolescence, turning a reasonable reward system into a voracious pleasure-seeking machine. Teenagers are biologically motivated to engage in behaviors that bring them pleasure. Basically, they are always chasing a high, which is why new experiences, risky decisions, and addictive behaviors seem so attractive to them.

So we send these amped-up, pleasure-oriented, ever-learning humans to school, and then we ask them what happened while they were there. Having some sense that they've learned a lot, yet lacking the ability to fully interpret all of the information their brains just took in, they become stuck. At the same time, they're bored to tears because the routine of school doesn't deliver the delicious dopamine kick that makes them feel good.

This is why amazing teachers have such a profound impact on us. Some educators and coaches are able to communicate new information in a way that's exciting and engaging. They also allow students creative space to process what they're learning in ways that are meaningful to them. They trigger teens' nucleus accumbens all over the place, and the students feel good.

These teachers cultivate desire. They understand that their work is only meaningful if they're forming students in a good way, not just keeping them entertained or stuffing them full of sterile information they don't care about. In his book *Desiring the Kingdom*, James K. A. Smith describes what education *should* be:

> Education is not something that traffics primarily in abstract, disembodied ideas; rather, education is a holistic endeavor that involves the whole person, including our bodies, in a process of formation that aims our desires, primes our imagination, and orients us to the world—all before we ever start thinking about it. This is why educational strategies that traffic only in ideas often fail to actually educate; that is, they fail to *form* people.[7]

Desire formation is at its peak during adolescence for another neurological reason. The adolescent brain trashes millions of unused synapses. Only the connections that get exercised through experience and education get to stay. Then the brain insulates those connections like the protective coating around high-voltage wires so teens won't lose their adolescent skills when they get older.

One of youth ministry's most popular concepts is that people are much more likely to make decisions about faith during their adolescent years than at any other point in their lives. Of course, people can adopt faith at any point in life; but teenage brains are specifically wired to retain a particular worldview, to be oriented around the desires they cultivated during adolescence.

Rather than being the prime season of life to indoctrinate students, adolescence is the developmental sweet spot for teens to figure out how they wish to see themselves and the world around them. Teenagers literally only think about the things that are most important and relevant to them. So a worldview that honors their desires and looks for ways that God is at work in the world is just as likely to stick with them as a worldview that doesn't take God into consideration at all.

Teenagers are predisposed to become whole people: becoming their unique selves, finding their tribe, and exploring their purpose. Therefore, the education of desire must be holistic, encompassing all aspects of adolescent development. The more we understand about the way teenagers are wired—physically, socially, psychologically—the better we'll be at connecting their desires to what God is doing in the world and helping them be their good selves more and more.

The same strategies that teachers and coaches use to humanize young people are precisely what advertising agencies and marketing consultants use to *dehumanize* them. Paying attention to trends in advertising offers us a fresh perspective on the widening gap between what teenagers crave and what they truly desire. Companies are figuring out how to ooze the trappings of teens' cravings under the guise of good desire, so these ravenous adolescent appetites will boost their bottom lines.

The advertising industry has a motto: "Kids Getting Older Younger." It's based on the idea that if you can hook someone on a product when she's a child or young teen, she will most likely stick with that product as an adult when her spending power is more significant than a monthly allowance.

Just like churches, businesses crumble when they stop being relevant to what people want. The lifeblood of most brands is to understand—or better, to *anticipate*—what teenagers want and then give it to them. And the church has the potential to regain this territory, if we pay attention.

Believe it or not, marketers are looking at what makes

religion work in order to make their advertising strategies even stronger. They're figuring out how to commoditize transcendent experiences, how to make their products feel like an encounter with the holy, because they understand that humans crave connection beyond themselves.

A neuromarketing company in the UK, Neurosense, has scanned people's brains to see which parts light up when they're shown different images.[8] They found that the same emotional part of the brain lights up when a person of faith (who also exhibits brand loyalty to the Apple company) is shown an image of an iPod or a Bible. In other words, a beautifully designed device that contains a person's soul put to music will push the same buttons in his brain as the holy book he's been trained to find himself in.

Advertising agencies understand the nuances of adolescent psychology and sociology. Teenagers often operate out of a sense of deprivation, as though their desires are irrelevant to others. They may feel unappreciated, unloved, overburdened, or overworked. Offering them a brand that oozes an abundance of love, peace, or confidence will do the trick.

Marketers know teenagers will shop to try to escape a sense of emptiness or to feel like they're in control. Consuming products and services will soothe their distorted sense of entitlement or make their stress abate for a few hours at the mall.

Branding professionals will trigger teenagers' emotions with cheap sensory tricks. Specific music, smells, and lighting inside the stores, along with constantly changing decor, makes the teenage brain light up with pleasure in a way that almost guarantees sales. The entire consumer process is engineered specifically to teenagers' developmental strengths and weaknesses.

They've figured out how to make just about anything sound like good news. See if the following scenario seems familiar:

> Mark works with teenagers. He goes to his guys' football games, grabs food with them on weekends, and talks with them about what they care about most. They invite him over to their homes all the time to hang with their family, eat meals, and play video games. Mark loves asking them about what they love and what they want out of life. He shares his life with the guys and is always willing to listen when they have suggestions. He is authentic, cool, and seems to want to know what they think. The guys really feel like Mark loves them.

If Mark is a youth pastor, he's gotten to know the guys in his small group better, and he's also looked for opportunities to get them to like him and accept Jesus.

If Mark is a marketer, he's just learned how his product's jingle should sound, what colors it should come in, how much it should cost, where these guys would be most likely to buy it, and who they hang out with who'd also be likely to buy one.

The experts of adolescent desire are not youth pastors but UGG, Apple, Starbucks, the creators of *Arrested Development*, and currently—the color teal. They employ the same tactics of relational connection as most youth ministries, with a degree of sophistication and intent that the church would never wish to mimic. It's like they're hunting teenagers.

Advertisers might glance at ways the church inspires devotion, but they hone in on the qualities that will give them the greatest return on their investment and then move along quickly. The machine of consumption is finely tuned to exploiting teenage desire in a way that compels devotion. "Our product will make you feel happy, hopeful, loved, beautiful, and ecstatic!" "This

brand will make your life an adventure!" "You don't
think about it, we've packaged it just for you!"

If the marketers can lure them in young, then they ju:
secure those synapses and gain a customer for life.

These marketing firms take everything we know about
adolescent development and formation, and they engineer
products and ad campaigns for teen consumption. In the
ad world there are three main categories of teenage desire,
and they just happen to correspond with the biggest tasks of
growing up: becoming yourself, figuring out who you belong
to, and exploring your purpose.

Sound familiar? These are good and necessary parts of growing
up. If you're looking to sell something, this is where you aim.

Teenagers have very few places where they can find help
with these three essential tasks. Family relationships are
tense or broken, schools are teaching to standardized tests,
extracurriculars are infused with college admission pressure,
and churches seem to have ulterior motives.

So brands swoop into the void and teach teens about love,
hope, and purpose. Since teenagers are just starting to flex their
ability to think abstractly, they are much more susceptible to
the promises of advertising. It's not hard to see how young
people feel invited into something bigger than themselves with
slogans like these:

There's an app for that. (Apple)
Touching is believing. (Apple)
Quality you can taste. (In-N-Out Burger)
The right to be real. (Converse)
You look nice today. (H&M)
Impossible is nothing. (Adidas)

reatness awaits. (Sony PlayStation)

Good marketing immediately confers a sense of authentic identity, participation in a bigger community, and an invitation to something epic. Teenagers with good desires to become themselves, find belonging, and figure out their purpose may have a tough time seeing through the fleeting promises of consumption.

The products that teenagers are most drawn to are the ones that speak to their deepest desires:

If I have this app, my life will be photo worthy. #nofilter #yolo
All of the girls on the soccer team wear those yoga pants. If I get them, I'll fit in.
If I hit Like, then—Poof!—kids in Africa will get clean water.

Rather than seeing companies as the enemy who competes with us for adolescents' attention ('cause let's be honest, the church is not much competition), how can we take the goodness they've articulated and offer students a version that is more substantial?

If the church consistently offered good news to young people about their identities, their communities, and their place in the world, then we could give iPods a run for their money.

Seriously.

The marketplace forms adolescents to be consumers who value relationships, differentiation, and a socially acceptable level of ethical consciousness.

Youth ministry seeks to form young people who are healthy, whole, and who desire to follow in the way of Jesus and participate in the work of the kingdom. It is the work of the church to speak into the fray, to quiet the voices that clamor to consume teenagers, and to speak peace to their good desires.

I've never seen a student turn down the real thing. They really do want good things, and they hate more than anything to be fooled or manipulated.

Yes, teenagers want a lot. But underneath their myriad cravings and momentary fixations are God-given desires that make them who they are, guide the way they live, and determine who they will become.

No wonder the Apple Store feels more like a cathedral than the church does. Apple devotes more time to figuring out what makes people feel as though they're at the intersection of transcendence and immanence. This magical, holy, desirable iPod? You can possess it; and in possessing it, maybe you can become more like it.

Every advertising executive, every company that succeeds does so because they've tapped into humanity's desires. It may look superficial to us, but they are revealing how teenagers are wired to want good things that will make them more human and more whole.

6
KINGDOM IMAGINATION

I didn't realize bikes came in pieces until I met my husband, Ian, a cycling enthusiast. Clearly I'm not mechanically minded. When Ian is working on his bikes, I'm always in charge of affixing the bottle cages, since they aren't crucial to the bike's function. It's safer this way.

Through a lot of questions and observation, I now understand that different bikes serve different purposes; and if you're serious about competing, then you need to have a road bike, track bike, mountain bike, time trial bike, commuter bike, and then another two or three bikes that you're working on for friends. We have a sort of vertical corral in our living room where Ian's bikes live, which appalls my mother and makes me proud of how urban and trendy my suburban self has become.

It's really important to me that I don't just tolerate this bike thing. Let me be clear: It is not my thing. I have a bike, just like I have a guitar—for occasional, embarrassing use.

We live in Seattle where you literally have to go uphill

both ways to go anywhere. This is basically my version of bike-riding hell. If Ian ever gets to live his dream of riding the famous bike race courses in Italy, we've already established that I will go find some bread, cheese, wine, and friendly Tuscan ponies to pet while he does his thing.

This is what happens when you're married and you love each other. You pay attention even when it's not your thing. I've gotten to the point where I can tell if a cyclist needs to raise or lower their bike seat, whether they need more gears, whether they have disc brakes, or if the frame is too big or too small for their height.

It's ridiculous, really. Some days I can't believe I devote brain cells to this trivia.

But love pays attention.

Ian loves bikes, so I love bikes for him. I don't lose myself in them, and the things I love aren't usurped by his passion. I just want to know what he cares about because I love knowing him so much. He comes alive when he rides his bike. The moment I walk in the door, I can tell whether or not he got to spin his legs that day. He looks like Eeyore if he misses a ride.

Riding bikes is such good news to him.
And I don't get it, personally.
But this is what love does.
It's always asking: "What is good news here, now, for this person?"

Like anything we love, good desires can get twisted and broken. For instance, sometimes Ian wants to win bike races more than it's good for him or for us. We have a constant trickle of gear flowing into and out of our lives—things like new sprockets that are supposed to work like a magical jetpack of speediness, or a more aerodynamic helmet.

Cycling has given Ian a lot of pride in what his body can do, but it also encourages some really unhealthy ways of viewing himself. The joke among his teammates is that you're skinny enough for racing once your loved ones stage an intervention. It's not funny; it's the dark side of desire.

This isn't sin in the common, traditional sense. It's disordered desire. Wanting to be healthy and fast are good desires, but they got twisted somewhere along the line. It doesn't make me want to shame Ian—shame is inherent in the problem itself. Instead, it breaks my heart.

My default question is: "What is good news for my husband right now?"

The funny thing is that the answer usually has something to do with Ian returning to his desire and trusting that it's good enough on its own. The solution is almost always to encourage him to return to what he loves about bikes—actually riding them. He's at his best when he is doing exactly what he wants and not worrying about new gear or changing his body to fit an unhealthy stereotype.

What is good news here, now, for this person or community? The gospel question always returns us to our true identity as people made in the image of God. And it can really only be asked if the subject is beloved. This is the question we ask when we truly love another person and we are trying our best to see the world through the lens of the kingdom.

It's an incredible act of love to exercise our imagination on behalf of someone else, to imagine the ways that the gospel could actually come true for them and offer them wholeness and life instead of brokenness and death.

The book of Luke tells a story about how the apostle Paul looked at the city of Athens with a kingdom imagination in Acts 17. But first, some historical and cultural background: In the ancient world, your well-being was connected to the gods' happiness. Families, businesses, and civic centers would literally carve out space for worship and offerings in the hope of pleasing the gods. On top of that, wealthy merchants, politicians, and military leaders often chose to show off their wealth and cultivate the people's good will by erecting grand temples to their god of choice.

Athens was already an ancient city by the time Paul got there. The Romans had conquered it and added it to their empire 200 years prior. With inclusion in the empire came a whole new roster of deities, Rome's gods as well as the religious beliefs of conquered people from the Mediterranean, North Africa, the Middle East, and Asia. Just as Athens was a melting pot churning with new ideas and curiosities, it was also a mosaic of devotion.

It's no wonder Paul was overwhelmed as he wandered through the streets. Everywhere he looked, there was another sanctuary dedicated to a particular god, or vendors selling animals for sacrifice, or the pious on their way to make offerings.

It probably seemed to be devoid of Paul's God. And Luke tells us Paul was distressed by what he saw. Then one day as he was exploring the city, he came across an altar dedicated "to an unknown god." This was how ancient people covered their bases, so to speak, in case there was a god they didn't know about and didn't want to anger. The altar served as a sort of placeholder for a god that hadn't been revealed yet.

This is the context of Paul's famous sermon to the Athenians in front of the Areopagus, or Mars Hill. He said:

"Athenians, I see how extremely religious you are in every way. For as I went through the city and looked carefully at the objects of your worship, I found among them an altar with the inscription, 'To an unknown god.' What therefore you worship as unknown, this I proclaim to you. The God who made the world and everything in it, [the God] who is Lord of heaven and earth, does not live in shrines made of human hands, nor is [God] served by human hands, as though [God] needed anything, since [God] gives to all mortals life and breath and all things. From one ancestor [God] made all nations to inhabit the whole earth, and [God] allotted the times of their existence and the boundaries of the places where they would live, so that they would search for God and perhaps grope for [God] and find [God]—though indeed [God] is not far from each one of us. For 'In [God] we live and move and have our being'; as even some of your own poets have said, 'For we too are his offspring.' (Acts 17:22–28)

Paul understood that good news and human desire go hand in hand. Your city doesn't become full of temples to the gods if you don't want to be connected with the divine. The people of Athens desired the presence of their gods.

Can you imagine what would have happened if Paul had approached the Athenians self-righteously, shaming them for their devotion to other gods and scaring them with the promise of an eternity in hell?

Fear and shame are indifferent.
Love pays attention.

Paul saw how religious the people were.
He looked carefully at their holy objects.
And in the midst of many gods, he found God.

Love pays attention.

Paul affirmed the people's search for God—they were doing exactly what they were made to do. Then, he shared the gospel: "God is not far from each one of us." Emmanuel. God with us. God with our God-given desires.

Paul even quoted their own poets! He read between the lines, affirming their goodness and their desire to search for truth, beauty, goodness, and life.

The Athenians didn't even know what they were naming, but they wanted to hold space for the possibility that there was more to their faith than they knew. Then Paul came along and said, "Yes! You have tasted the truth! And the truth has a name."

This is how we gospel. (Yes, we just made *gospel* a verb.)

One of the most pastoral things we can do is help students recognize the ways they've already made space for God to show up in their lives. We get to help them see where they've raised up altars to an unnamed God, and then encourage them to find language for the spirituality they already have.

Because *all* of life is spiritual, not just the stuff that happens before an altar. As we follow God, perhaps we get to take unknown altars and repurpose them for the mysterious, living, Triune God.

I wonder what Paul would say if he walked through the local high school today? Where would he find young people "searching for God, perhaps reaching out and finding God"?

Students of High School! I see how extremely affectionate you are in every way. For as I walked through your hallways and observed your interactions with each other, there were many public displays of affection. What you crave with your bodies, I proclaim to you. The God who made the world and everything in it, including your hormones, created you to experience love. This God is love, and God made you to seek and find love that is real and eternal. Even as one of your own prophets, Suzanne Collins, has said, "'You love me. Real or not real?' I tell him, 'Real.'"[9]

Students of High School! I see how extremely stressed you are in every way. For as I scrolled through your Facebook posts and your tweets, there were cries of exhaustion and prayers for relief from the pressure. What you long for in your lament, I proclaim to you. The Lord of heaven and earth created you to work hard, play hard, and rest well. This God is the Prince of Peace, and God made you to seek and find life instead of the stress which leads to death. Even as one of your own poets, Tina Fey, has said, "I was a little excited but mostly blorft. 'Blorft' is an adjective I just made up that means 'Completely overwhelmed but proceeding as if everything is fine and reacting to the stress with the torpor of a possum.'"[10]

Students of High School! I see how extremely technological you are in every way. For as I walked through the cafeteria, I saw a sea of blue faces bent over glowing screens. What you long for in your insatiable connectivity, I proclaim to you. The God who gives everyone life, breath, and all things created you to make eye contact with others. Though we are all different, God made humans to be in community with one another, so they would search for God together and perhaps reach out and find God—though God is not far from any one of us. For even as your own artist,

Bob Marley, has said, "As it was in the beginning (One Love!); So shall it be in the end (One Heart!)."[11]

What we do shows us what we want.
When what we want has even a hint of goodness, love, beauty, truth, or life to it, it reveals our desire for God.

When we love another person or a community, we take the time to understand what they love. As we observe and learn and train ourselves, we're able to pick out the kingdom of God that is already in their midst, revealed in what they want that is true, good, beautiful, loving, and full of life.

Following Jesus is about seeing the world through kingdom-colored lenses.

Do the words *evangelism* and *mission* stress you out?

I confess they totally freak me out because they come with so much baggage. As a teenager, I went to youth group at a seeker-sensitive megachurch. They were all about getting us to bring our friends to church to hear about Jesus. It felt like so much pressure. I would strategically invite friends to events that I knew were primarily fun and lighter on the come-to-Jesus. It seemed too contrived to me, like I was tricking them into faith by luring them into our loud, rocking, flashy auditorium.

Out in the church lobby, there were benches situated beneath some artificial trees, like the places where you tend to see bored men sitting in the mall. The senior pastor nicknamed them the "Fools' Benches" because church members would invite friends or family to church and then wait for them on those benches. Sometimes the invitees didn't show up, leaving the believer feeling very noble and a little foolish.

It took a long time for me to stop feeling guilty about not inviting people to church. Inviting them to the kingdom has been so much more fun—and frankly, more foolish!

The most popular understandings of *mission* mean either that people must come to a church and hear about God, or we must take God to "them" out in the "world" (basically anywhere that isn't a church building).

There is more and more momentum building behind the idea of reclaiming the concept of mission as being a way of revealing God where God is already at work. This is what Paul did on Mars Hill. He set up a paradigm for us to look at the world around us and figure out where God already is.

I wonder if the most foolish thing we can do is see God where others don't and look at the world through kingdom-colored lenses.

There is something of God's presence in everything good, true, loving, beautiful, and living. Even that which is unhealthy, broken, sinful, or evil is the result of good desire gone awry.

The most compelling Christians I know are those who suspend their judgment and walk through the world openly because they know love has nothing to fear. They love others so completely that they're willing to posture themselves as students, learning stories and asking curious questions instead of bulldozing people with a religious opinion.

Their eyes are big, taking in everything that hints at God.
Their hands are open, ready to hold people when they forget they are good.
They are attuned to the signs of good desire.
They are quick to love.
They embody good news.

Looking at the world through kingdom-colored lenses means we are on the lookout for ways that God is already present wherever we go. The world looks different when we take Jesus at his word: the kingdom of heaven is near.

What if we believed our own prayer? Thy kingdom come, on earth as it is in heaven.

What if we believed right along with the psalmist that the earth is full of the presence of God?

What if everything that we thought was idolatry was actually disordered, misplaced desire for the kingdom of God?

Instead of finding God in the midst of a finely tuned worship service or a three-point sermon, seeing the world through kingdom-colored lenses means we start to encounter God in the mess and ambiguity of life. Every day. All the time.

Unless this is the way you were trained to see the world, adopting this perspective takes some practice.

My first time was at a Taylor Swift concert with 10,000 teenage girls. I cannot describe the ear-splitting pitch they achieved with their excited screams. They made me feel middle-aged at age 24. But the concert was totally fun, and as a youth pastor I was mostly entertained by the senseless devotion of the young fans around us.

Then Taylor sang a song with a hallelujah chorus. Suddenly, there's no more screaming, just thousands of young voices singing:

> *Because these things will change*
> *Can you feel it now?*
> *These walls that they put up to hold us back will fall*

down
It's a revolution, the time will come
For us to finally win
And we'll sing hallelujah, we'll sing hallelujah.[12]

I wept as my eyes scanned the arena, taking in the slow sway of blue screens raised with solidarity. Singing hallelujah.

They didn't come to Jesus, I know that. It wasn't an altar call; it was a concert. But something about the song and the moment struck them. And whether they know it or not, they were swimming in holiness. *Hallelujah*—praise God—resonated in them, even if they couldn't articulate it that way.

What does good news look like for them? Singing hallelujah with Taylor Swift, being reminded that they will finally win over whatever is holding them back. How is this not the gospel?

The world is saturated with the gospel when we see it through the lens of the kingdom. I've now become that woman who stops in the middle of a cracked sidewalk to read spray-painted utility instructions or altruistic graffiti on parking signs:

I'm a Midwestern girl at heart, so attending a professional sporting event has always meant baseball. As it turns out, Seattle's MLB team is a little depressing to watch. (Sorry, Mariners.) So I've found myself turning, along with the entire city, toward Major League Soccer and the magic that is the Seattle Sounders Football Club.

We love the Sounders. And when I go to the games, I learn about worship.

The diehard fans' kingdom is at the south end of the stadium. It's a mythical place—a choreographed sea of green, blue, and grey. Everyone stands the whole game. And they have a hymnal of sorts.

Two people lead the liturgy, taking turns facing the stands and calling out songs, chants, and motions. They call; the people respond. The most devoted fans know the songs by heart, while new converts (me) follow along with awkward eagerness, wanting so badly to fit in.

One song is called "The Blue and the Green." They sing*:

> Go Sounders go!
> Fight Sounders fight!
> **And the entire world will tremble at your might!**
> **We sing for you!**
> **We love you so!**
> **And we will follow you wherever you may go!**
> **Where you may go!**
> We are the blue! **We are the blue!**
> We are the green! **We are the green!**
> We are the ECS and you can hear us scream! **Hear us scream!**
> For our boys! **For our boys!**
> Until the end! **'Til the end!**
> Our love for you only the gods can understand!
> **Can understand!**

*The regular font is for the leader; the **bold** font is for everyone, just like in worship.*

What do you hear in this song?
Where are these fans expressing desire?
Do you see anything good, true, loving, beautiful, or alive in this chant?
How can you imagine God is already present?
Is there a place where God is missing?
What is good news for these people?

The apostle Paul might say:

> Fans of the Sounders! I see how extremely devoted you
> are in every way. For as I sat in the stadium and listened
> carefully to your liturgies, I found among you a love
> that only the gods can understand. What therefore you
> worship as the Sounders, this I proclaim to you. God
> made people to be co-creators with God, participants
> in bringing heaven to earth. This God is Love, and
> understands your devotion only because God loves you
> more than you can imagine. God is not far from your
> chanting. For as your own poets have said, "We sing for
> you! We love you so! And we will follow you wherever
> you may go!"

Love pays attention to the beloved's good news—and takes
it seriously. We imagine on others' behalf what the kingdom
could look like.

In the kingdom brokenness is made whole.
The dead are brought back to life.
Hunger is fed.
Thirst is quenched.
The wounded are healed.
The lost are found.
Those who were trapped are set free.

Can you imagine what good news looks like for your
students—and then invite them into it?

This is what good youth pastors do.

We pay attention to what our students love because we love
them. Then we connect what they love with who God is
because we hope they will find that it is good news to follow in
the way of Jesus.

7

YOUTH PASTORS ARE PASTORS TOO

I know the way you can get
When you have not had a drink of Love:
Your face hardens,
Your sweet muscles cramp.
Children become concerned
About a strange look that appears in your eyes
Which even begins to worry your own mirror
And nose.

Squirrels and birds sense your sadness
And call an important conference in a tall tree.
They decide which secret code to chant
To help your mind and soul.

Even angels fear that brand of madness
That arrays itself against the world
And throws sharp stones and spears into
The innocent
And into one's self.

O I know the way you can get
If you have not been drinking Love:

You might rip apart
Every sentence your friends and teachers say,
Looking for hidden clauses.

You might weigh every word on a scale
Like a dead fish.

You might pull out a ruler to measure
From every angle in your darkness
The beautiful dimensions of a heart you once
Trusted.

I know the way you can get
If you have not had a drink from Love's
Hands.

That is why all the Great Ones speak of
The vital need
To keep remembering God,
So you will come to know and see Him
As being so Playful
and Wanting,

Just Wanting to help . . .

—Hafiz, "I Know the Way You Can Get"

The last time a church offered me a youth pastor job, I cried.

All through seminary I worked with a church I loved. I had a chance to build a youth ministry from scratch—a youth pastor's dream. Unfortunately, our senior pastor created an environment where the staff felt like cogs in a ministry machine. We were meant to be indestructible, constantly "on," and ultimately dispensable. Success meant having more programs or events to announce at the weekly staff meeting, and always working more hours than you were compensated for without question or complaint.

As I prepared to graduate, which would ideally have been the time to secure employment, I resigned. It was heartbreaking; everyone I spoke to agreed that I was a great fit for my students and for the church community. I just wasn't a good match for my boss.

I spent the summer applying for any job I could find. I even took a metro bus driver test before I realized they were hiring temporary help to navigate the Seattle rush hour. The job options are limited when all you've ever done is youth ministry and the economy is struggling.

Finally, St. Andrew's Episcopal Church in Seattle invited me to interview. I thought I might be a great fit for them, theologically and philosophically. They also seemed like a community where I might be able to lick my wounds and heal.

When Father Peter called to offer me the position, I was excited and also a little hesitant. Did they understand that while I'd been a youth pastor for 10 years, I'd never done children's ministry? Were they open to forming students by connecting teenagers' desires to what God is already doing in the world?

Pete invited me to his home to discuss my questions. If I'd learned anything from my previous church experience, it was that clarifying expectations is far easier on the *front* end of a ministry relationship than at the bloody end. I expected that we'd go through strategic ministry planning, compare my vision to his vision, and eventually come to an understanding of whether I was a good fit for what he had in mind.

121

Do you know that feeling you get when you take a sip from a cool glass of water and then just keep on drinking because you didn't realize how thirsty you were or how delicious water could be? That's how it felt the first time Pete pastored me.

We spoke about how God formed us as pastors. He said he was looking for someone like me to lead him in loving and serving St. Andrew's young people. Pete invited me to speak to ministry desires I didn't even know I had. His first act of pastoring me was to create space for me to be myself and be affirmed for who I am, rather than what I can produce.

I felt so honored. Of course I accepted the job. It had been too long since I'd felt like a youth pastor and a person at the same time. And that's when, with a big smile on his face, he handed me a huge rainbow of paint chips and said, "We'd love to paint your office before you start. Just let me know what color you'd like."

That simple gesture broke me in the way that only too much kindness can. Cue the tears. And paint my office teal, please.

This is what pastors do. (Not make you cry—well, sometimes.) A good pastor names that which we'd hoped was true all along: that we are good and that we're enough. A good pastor holds on to the reality of the gospel for us when we can't dare to believe that it's true for us too.

We don't know each other, but I believe in you.

You lack nothing.
You already have everything you need to be a good youth worker.
You reveal God to your students in a way no one else ever has, or can, or will.
You're not *just* a youth worker. You're a pastor.

You love and like your students.
You're doing your best to follow in the way of Jesus.
You lack nothing.

There is so much pressure on youth workers to have it all figured out so we can be a good example for the young people in our care. If we do let our weaknesses show, they need to be carefully engineered as illustrations or teachable moments so students catch a glimpse of our authenticity and learn from our mistakes.

We often talk about how God "uses" us in the lives of students, or how God wants to "use" students to do the work of the kingdom (or, I might add, "using" the Bible to prove a point). Language like this sets us up to be objects of convenience instead of people in relationship; it destroys desire for the sake of obligation.

Who would ever believe that Love uses the Beloved?

If I told you I use my husband for washing dishes, you'd think I was a callous, calculating monster-woman. You never speak about using someone you love.

We are made to be resurrection stories, not sermon illustrations or objects to be used.

We are people with broken desires who name sin, injustice, and violence as we follow in the way of Jesus' crucifixion.

We are people with good desires who name life, truth, goodness, and beauty as we follow in the way of Jesus' resurrection and ascension.

Pastoring students means leading out of our wholeness and brokenness, not just the spiffed-up dirty bits that can be used to prove God's point. If we only set an example of the way things should be instead of the way things really are, we do a lot of harm. We don't live in a world that is as it should be; we live in this messy reality. So the best we can do is invite teenagers to watch us live—in faith and doubt—as we do our best to follow in the way of Jesus and participate in the work of the kingdom. It's pastoral work to hold hope and love on behalf of others. That's what we mean when we talk about incarnating Jesus or incarnating the gospel—that we embody the good news in the midst of others, hoping it will connect to their hearts' desires.

Sometimes I wonder if I'll ever believe the good news for myself as much as I believe it for my students. There is no doubt in my mind that God desires wholeness, restoration, and reconciliation for everyone, and that God is at work in teenagers' good desires to make earth more like heaven. I just have to admit that as ardently as I hold these things for others, I struggle to trust that they're also true for me. Do you ever feel like that?

The gospel is for us.
Life from death is for us.
Desire is for us, too.
It's just so easy to forget.

When did you give up on wanting good things? Which of your dreams sit on dusty shelves, canned and long forgotten? Something happened. Someone said something that convinced you that what you wanted wasn't good—or if it was, you'd never be good enough to deserve it. Somewhere in that process, you gave up on desire. Unfulfilled desires become hateful to us in that specific and poisonous way you hate someone that you used to love, someone who promised to never betray you.

Often we become aware of the desires we've silenced when we experience something that moves us. Emotions tend to bring unrequited desire bubbling to the surface.

A song comes on the radio and hits you right in the feelings.
The words of a prayer speak to you in a way you didn't expect.
A stranger's kindness overwhelms you.
The lines of a poem stop you in your tracks: "I know the way you can get, when you have not had a drink of Love."[13]

Discovering long-lost desire feels good and it feels painful, like you finally remembered that you lost something really important to you. Tuning in to your desires might break your heart. But it will also invite you into the abundant life you were created for. We weren't made to run on empty. This is how we become whole: We learn to bring every part of ourselves—the parts we like and the parts we don't—to come and play and see what God will do.

Maybe this is why Jesus exhorts people to become like little children. Kids are the best at desire. They are uninhibited in all their wanting because they haven't yet learned to be ashamed of their desires. Children know how to reflect the presence of the One Who Desires; maybe this is why they have such wild and wonderful imaginations. As we get older, we have to be taught how to desire what is desirable—not because we're sinful, but because the broken world has taught us to forget. It's almost like it's been beaten out of us.

So what do *you* want?
Another way to ask this is, "What makes you feel most fully alive?"
How do these desires draw you into God's presence?

These are the questions that form us most meaningfully. We are formed by desire more than anything else. Desire isn't just for students. If we want to help spiritually form our students according to their desires, then we may need to spend some time with our own desires—the ones that are alive and well, and also the ones that have broken our hearts. The most meaningful thing we can offer our students is to let them see us do our best to follow Jesus with our whole selves.

I decided to be a youth pastor when I was 18. During my rebellious senior year in high school, I convinced my mom to let me skip school for a couple of days so I could attend our church's student ministry conference. (I know, I was wild.) I went through a great undergraduate youth ministry program on the East Coast, and all the while I served in churches as an intern or worked as a teaching assistant for the youth ministry department. I studied everything: history, teaching, formation, leadership, counseling, mission trips, theology, and evangelism. I studied a lot, but my real learning didn't begin until I started working full time with teenagers after I graduated.

It turns out that students don't remember most of what their youth pastor says.
No one told me that.
It makes sense though. How many of our own talks do we remember?

We remember the things that are most meaningful to us. Maybe we don't remember a particular conversation, or sermon, or question verbatim, but we remember the spirit, the substance of what was said that changed us. The things that connect to whatever our heart's desire is at a given moment are the things that stick with us and form us into people. Timing and connecting to desire are everything. Our formation is cumulative over a lifetime of these moments. This is how we make people in the regular world, not just Christians in the church.

There is no way to predict what will stick at any given moment. All that is asked of us is that we be faithful, love our students well, and try to create space where students can become aware of how they experience God.

One of my favorite students (you have favorites too, so don't judge me) made it a habit to check in with me weekly about her relationship with God during her high school years. One week she'd say, "God and I are doing great! He finally showed up, and I even prayed a little." And the very next week she might say something like, "I don't believe *anything* this week. This terrible thing happened and I don't think God cares at all."

This is the *best*!
It means she is continually wrestling with God and being honest about it.

Teenagers don't need a shiny, packaged faith. They don't need canned questions that fish for easy, predetermined answers. The best thing we can offer students is ourselves. We can give them our presence and let them see the ways that we try and fail to follow in the way of Jesus.

Students remember the stuff that matters.
They remember the relationships that bring them life, love, and encouragement.
They remember the experiences that make them feel alive and known.
Your students, most of all, remember *you*.

To students, the best youth pastor in the world is the one who is *theirs*. They don't know there are youth ministry professionals who write books and blogs, speak at conferences and retreats, or offer coaching and consulting. They literally have no idea that youth ministry is a profession. They only know *you*.
The best youth pastor they could ever have is the one who is

there—and that's you.

You're not there to be Jesus to them. That is a narcissistic abuse of the concept of incarnational ministry. You're there to be *you* with them and let them watch you as you do your best to follow in the way of Jesus. This makes you kind of a big deal.

You already have everything you need to love them well.

Think about that for a few minutes. Go for a walk and think about how good you are at loving your students. If you need something to jog your memory, reread notes from kids who've thanked you for being there for them, or emails from parents who adore you. Seriously. Stop reading and remember how good you are.

Your students will remember you.

We form others as we were formed.
Who formed you?
Who comes to mind as a person who helped you to desire God?

I remember who those people were in my life, though years and distance have now separated us.

Deborah was my middle school small group leader, the victim of our overwhelming awkwardness. She loved us when we first started meeting and we girls wouldn't talk, and she still loved us months later when she couldn't get us to *stop* talking.

Janice was my mentor who treated me like a real person and never failed to encourage me to pursue the good things I wanted. She had an insatiable love for life and always spoke the truth.

Jayne, Jackie, and Andrea invited me into their women's small group, their conversations, and their lives. They offered me dignity by inviting me to contribute my ideas and taking my desires seriously, even though I was so young.

I remember being loved and being drawn to Jesus because of that love. These dear people cared about my desires and helped give me language to connect all that love and goodness to God. Their example and acceptance made me want to follow Jesus. They pastored me by being who they were. They weren't just doing their jobs. They were being themselves without any ulterior motives.

I'm not concerned that anyone become a better youth pastor. I'm concerned that we become more whole people and bring that experience to our students—because that's the part that matters most. When I speak about wholeness, I don't mean perfection. By "whole" I mean how we bring every piece of ourselves, all of our desires, into our pastoral work.

Because youth pastors are pastors too.

One of the church's first pastors was the apostle Peter. He's my favorite of all the disciples, mostly because he's so wonderfully human. Over and over we see him living in tune with his desires, even when they get him in trouble. So it makes sense that desire would be a theme in his letter to believers across the Roman Empire. He writes:

> Dear friends, I urge you, as foreigners and exiles, to abstain from sinful desires, which wage war against your soul. Live such good lives among the pagans that, though they accuse you of doing wrong, they may see your good deeds and glorify God on the day [God] visits us. (1 Peter 2:11–12, NIV)

Again, that's not the version I typically hear in the evangelical church. Usually it goes something like this:

> Dear friends, as good Christians persecuted by this secular world, run away from your desires, which are immoral and wage war against your soul. Live such a morally upright life that people will be jealous of you and accuse you of being in the wrong, but you'll be proven right by God when God comes one day to judge them.

The actual text raises some questions for me.

What if Peter was speaking to the complexity of desire? What if he understood that sometimes the good desires God gave us get twisted and wage war against our good souls?

By "such good lives," I wonder if Peter meant lives that are saturated by desires that lead to life, love, goodness, beauty, and truth. Maybe he's talking about living the kind of good life that people would actually want, not the morally impeccable existence that will make them judge us—or assume we're judging them.

I wonder if desire that's oriented around the kingdom has to look wrong to a lot of people because the kingdom doesn't make a lot of sense. Desiring restoration can seem like the wrong and foolish thing sometimes. I don't blame people for judging. Sometimes I judge myself for this weird hope.

Peter never calls desire bad. He just asks that we run away from things which serve death and run toward that which serves life. His pastoral task is to invite people to live the best kind of lives—so good that even those who don't know God will want to glorify God.

Live such good lives.

Goodness speaks to desire in a way that rightness never can. We are youth pastors, and we are pastors. The apostle Peter's advice is to recognize those desires that don't bring us life and lean into the ones that do. Everyone wants good things, and that goodness just might lead us all into the presence of God.

This is our pastoral work. Live such a good life that you draw people to God. You can't have too much of a good life. We do a disservice to ourselves and the lives we were made for if we orient ourselves around just trying to be right and perfect all the time. Or if we buy into the idea that we aren't "real pastors." We've allowed ourselves to be dehumanized, stripped of our desire.

We need each other.

Can we be honest about what it's like to be a youth pastor among other youth pastors? Maybe I'm sensitive about this because I'm a woman and I'm typically in the minority. I admit that I sometimes feel like I'm on the fringe of some secret brotherhood, and I don't know the right handshake.

The performance anxiety in some of these networking contexts can suffocate me.
We're all guilty of humble bragging.
Our desire to be seen and reassured that we aren't failing robs us of a safe space to be humans together.

I really don't want to hear about your Fourth of July outreach where 325 teens showed up for an overnighter at an awesome amusement park, and a Christian band performed live, and it didn't cost the students anything to attend because your operating budget is more than I make in a year, and isn't it great how the church supports the youth?

If I were perfect, I would be so excited for you. But due to a failure of my personality and because I'm only human (or maybe a little jealous), I have to wonder if you had even one meaningful interaction with a kid that entire night, or if all that was left the next day were some Facebook statuses or Instagram pictures buried in a newsfeed somewhere.

Just walking through the exhibit hall at a national convention or regional conference is usually enough to send me spiraling into a deep depression. National conferences set up acres of booths, and all these organizations are there to demonstrate and talk about all of the stuff we "need" to be good youth pastors. If I attend, I have to avoid the vendors area. They're not offering bad things, but they're not offering essential things either. I feel hunted, not empowered.

We sometimes confuse resources and gimmicks for youth ministry. We get stuck thinking that if we had just the right icebreaker, group game, small-group discussion guide, or pop culture illustration—then maybe our teens would love Jesus. I must confess that I pretty much think ice blocking and Nooma videos have magical properties.

But this is not the way formation works. This isn't the way people become people, even. It's sort of unnatural, really. Most of what we learn our whole lives happens in the context of relationships, dialogue, and interaction with others instead of in formal learning environments.

There is no magic-bullet curriculum that will bring unchurched kids to your church. There is no surefire talk outline that will bring them to Jesus. There is no perfect ministry calendar, no retreat of instant gratification.

Students aren't formed by a predictable system, constant programmatic steps, or purpose-driven blueprints. They don't move linearly from one stage of spiritual maturity to another, like ranks in the military or ballplayers rounding the bases. I dream of gathering with other youth pastors and getting to know each other as people, not just professionals.

What if we actually talked with each other about our desires?

If I were meeting with my colleagues and felt invited to talk about my heart's desires, I might be able to tell the stories that make me who I am. Maybe I could finally tell you all that sometimes I wish I'd learned about horses instead of teenagers so I could run away and work on a ranch someplace where the sky is big and I could be thin, strong, and tan.

Maybe other youth pastors dread going back to church for youth group after a long day, but they absolutely love it once they get there. Then I might not feel so guilty and alone.

What if we were honest and a little bit vulnerable?

Maybe we could speak about the ways we see God, and how we're so disappointed when we don't.

Sometimes it feels like all youth pastors talk about is preparing to pastor instead of actual acts of pastoring.

What if we shared about our encounters with students, not just how our programs and plans are going?

What if we checked in about this work we love rather than how we make frameworks that we hope will give us opportunities to do the work we love?

And I could hear about how you talked with Jeremy about his parents' divorce, and you could hear about how Andrea finally decided to quit the gymnastics team because she hates it and she's going to paint instead.

It would be so good.

We don't have to be so alone, even when we get together. We could offer each other a diet of compassion instead of competition.

I'd rather tell you about how Ryan shared that his favorite part about God is the mystery, and how he spent his solo time on the retreat watching a cloud dissipate from the sky. He thinks his faith would be stronger if he had a big, transcendent experience of God. I'd share how I got to ask him if he sees any connection between God's mystery, a disappearing cloud, and experiencing God. And then I'd share how a Frisbee flew over our heads and he ran off to get it.

Desire means evaluating our ministries qualitatively, through stories of how students are discovering that the good news is good for them, here and now.

It means we trade the numbers, which are irrelevant and measurable, for the most relevant and immeasurable—stories of formation and love.

Reorienting our lives and ministries around desire is risky because it means discipleship happens organically, and not always in ways we can expect or explain.

This kind of ministry isn't sexy, as far as ministry goes. Orienting our lives and our work around humanity and desire is not glamorous.

We live in a world, and often serve a church, which places value on tangible outcomes. It's so much easier to take attendance and count conversions than to figure out how our students are growing in their love and their desire for God. I have no idea how to do that. I only know it when I see it.

Not everybody recognizes the value of adolescents' desire. Many are scared of it, or afraid of what it will do to others' perceptions of the church. Sometimes setting a new vision for ministry that deals honestly with spiritual formation means that not everyone wants to come along; students, parents, staff, congregants, elders, or even the senior pastor may take issue with movement away from the status quo.

It gets further complicated when your ministry is connected to your income and your community. Many youth pastors were hired to do a specific job, usually in a way the church already had in mind.

We hear familiar language in job descriptions at churches across the country, and the following is adapted from an actual job listing I found on the Internet:

> Community Church is a fast-growing community with a need to reach lost teenagers. The youth pastor will be responsible for the oversight of all ministry to students in 6th through 12th grades. Our ministry includes, but is not limited to, a weekly service for junior high on Sundays, Wednesday night services for junior high and high school, small groups, events, and outreach. The youth pastor is responsible to recruit, train, and develop volunteers for the ministry. Outreach and leadership development will be a core priority for our new youth pastor. Staff responsibilities include attending weekly team meetings, participating in church events, and performing other duties as assigned by the senior pastor.

> The ideal candidate will have a proven track record of working in a large church setting and being committed to reaching non-Christians with a high degree of

innovation, recruitment, and retention of new teenagers. Proven experience in creative programming, music, and problem solving is vital. Work history that includes communication and leadership is a must. Finally, the successful candidate will be ready to go, to "plug and play" from day one on the job.

Oh, church. You break our hearts.
When did you turn your pastors into ministry machines?
How did your desire for the kingdom become craving for the empire?
Did you really just ask a human being, one who's charged with caring for a community as a pastor, to "plug and play"?
This doesn't set up anyone for success.

Is this why any of us became youth workers?
What do we say when people ask why we do what we do?

We say names. We name the people who saved us through meaningful encounters and by connecting us to the good news. We don't talk about how our youth pastor was so great because she had a proven track record of innovation, recruitment, and retention.

Clearly there needs to be some sort of structure in order for ministry to happen. At some point it's helpful to get people together, and that definitely requires some kind of gathering. But the gathering isn't the point. We get together because we trust that when we gather, God is present in a profound way, and we can call forth goodness from each other in a way we can't do alone. We gather so we can remind each other of what is good, true, beautiful, and lovely—and so we can create more gospel together.

What is your real job description—the stuff that's important to you?

Mine would read something like this:

> St. Andrew's is an Episcopal church in the Greenlake neighborhood of Seattle, seeking someone to faithfully pastor our students and their families. We're looking for a person who loves students and is doing her best to follow in the way of Jesus. Our hope is that students, families, and our whole community would learn to name their good desires and see how they are connected to the reconciliation of all things. We want her to invite our church, but especially teenagers, to embody the good news of the gospel in meaningful ways in our neighborhood. We'd love it if youth group were a place where our children could become more whole and more human as they explore what it means to seek God, be found by God, and participate in bringing the kingdom of heaven to earth. Pastoral responsibilities include faithful presence, open communication, and a commitment to spiritual direction and/or professional support networks.
>
> The successful candidate will be authentic in her brokenness and goodness. She will be invested in healthy relationships that encourage and challenge her. She will ask many questions and be comfortable with not knowing all the answers. Welcoming of everyone is a must. She needs to be ready to hold her plans loosely and play with us from day one, according to the good desires of the community.

This feels human. It feels like the church wants a youth pastor who is a pastor, not just a cog in a big, churning ministry machine.

Desire can be a professional liability. I'm not good at the ol' "Plug & Play," and I sort of lost my job for orienting my ministry around desire. I was working at a church where the senior pastor was really concerned about growth and public perception. It seemed like he wanted to be famous for pastoring more than he wanted to actually pastor. Our youth group wasn't growing at a braggable pace. My presence on social media wasn't polished. We didn't have a ton of events and didn't do outreach evangelism.

Instead, our students talked about the highs and lows of life, and what they desired. We asked questions we didn't know the answers to, and we tried to figure out how to love each other even though we were so, so different. I've never felt more whole as a pastor, and I've never seen students more eager to connect with God's presence.

This was not the stuff of fame.
It was the stuff of life. I think it's how we make each other into people.

This is what I want to invite students into.
Because this is the kind of God-saturated life I desperately desire for myself.

What do you want for yourself? It matters.

8
WILD GOOSE CHASE

Whether you turn to the right or to the left,
your ears will hear a voice behind you
saying, "This is the way; walk in it."
—Isaiah 30:21, NIV

A long time ago on the banks of the Jordan River, Jesus was baptized by his cousin John, a crazy-looking itinerant preacher. The gospel writers tell us that when John lifted Jesus from the water, the heavens parted and Jesus saw the Spirit of God descend on him in the bodily form of a dove. A voice like rolling thunder accompanied this vision: "This is my Son, whom I love; with him I am well pleased."

I can't think of a voice I'd rather have students hear and believe.

This is my daughter.
This is my son.
I love him/her.
I'm pleased with him/her.

Honestly, I have trouble believing it for myself on all but my best days.

It's just like the Spirit of God to remind us that we are good. I don't know what it was like for Jesus to grow up—whether or not he knew he was divine. But I'm sure he was keenly aware of humanity's brokenness by the time he stepped into that river.

I wonder whom the Spirit was talking to.
Maybe the message is for the benefit of the crowd and Jesus already knew without a doubt that he is God's Son who is loved and pleasing.

But what if the voice was a reminder for Jesus? We speak about how Jesus became human so he'd go through everything we humans go through firsthand. Could it be that Jesus experienced doubt or needed reassurance about his identity? He got tired, angry, and frustrated, after all. Maybe Jesus needed to be reminded that he was made in the image of God, dearly loved, and good and pleasing to his Father.

Over and over throughout Scripture and history, we become aware of the Spirit when s/he calls us to be the whole, beautiful, desiring people we were created to be, so we can participate with God in restoring the world. When human beings were first created, God breathed breath and spirit into our bodies and called us good. The Spirit is the voice that reminds us we are good and we are made to want good things. S/he calls us to return to our true identities when the world is broken and our desires are misdirected.

We need the Spirit for desire. S/he is vital to how we're formed into whole people who follow in the way of Jesus. S/he helps us see the thin places where heaven and earth collide, and s/he is present with us as we mourn when our world is a living hell. The Holy Spirit invites our good desires to collaborate in the reconciliation of all things that Jesus spoke about.

I believe all of that to be true; but again, it's a part of my theology that is written in pencil. I hold it loosely, expecting that I have no idea what to expect when it comes to the Holy Spirit.

Talking about the Spirit is tricky because everyone's experience is unique. When I say *Spirit*, I probably mean something completely different than you do. No one has a monopoly on understanding this person of the Trinity, although many theologians have offered helpful insights throughout church history. As the church engages the Holy Spirit, she reveals the beautiful diversity—and occasional confusion—of the body of Christ.

Every denomination has a different way of engaging with the Spirit. It works out pretty well, actually, because no one can fully grasp what s/he is like or how s/he works. Some find the greatest expression of their faith in relation to the Spirit; others limit their engagement to a nod of acknowledgement at Pentecost. Youth ministries often keep their distance from the Spirit; it seems much easier for young people to grasp God the Father or Jesus the Son than the nebulous, ambiguous Divine Presence/Wind Breath that is the third person of the Trinity.

Our students will pick up on what *we* believe, like it or not. What do you think about when you think about the Spirit?

Maybe you think about a feeling of peace.
Maybe signs, wonders, and miracles come to mind.
Maybe you immediately think about speaking in tongues.
Maybe the Spirit reminds you of worship music.
Or maybe the Spirit is a nudge toward social justice or repentance.

Depending on your personal experience or faith tradition, the Spirit might evoke feelings of fear, peace, confusion, conviction, amusement, or transcendence. S/he makes me feel *all* of these feelings.

What we believe about the Holy Spirit is our pneumatology, and if we're orienting ourselves and our ministries around adolescent desire, then we need to consider how we believe God shows up in the world.
Who is the Holy Spirit?
What does the Spirit do?
How does it matter?

Like us, the writers of Scripture seem a little disoriented by their experiences of the Spirit.

At creation the Spirit hovered over the waters and participated in making everything good. It makes me think maybe the Spirit is a little like Bob Ross, flitting back and forth across the globe, creating all of the "happy little trees" with a calm voice.[14]

For the Israelites, the Spirit was present in the Shekinah glory that dwelled first in the tabernacle and then later in the temple. The Spirit stuck to people as a blinding glow after they'd had a close encounter with holiness. And apparently the Spirit is transferrable between people, leaving some and going to others (Numbers 11:17).

The book of Judges insists that God's Spirit "rushes upon" people, sometimes in violent ways. (Check out the story of Samson in Judges 14 and 15.)

The first book of Samuel prefers the words "prophetic frenzy" to describe the way the Spirit communicates through would-be prophets. (Read the story of Saul in 1 Samuel 10 in the NRSV.) First Samuel also describes how an "evil spirit from the Lord" entered Saul and wreaked havoc on his personal and communal life (1 Samuel 16). I can't explain that one. How God can have anything to do with evil is a question for another book and a more savvy author.

The prophets held an eschatological hope and vision of a day when God's Spirit would be "poured out" on all people (Isaiah 44; Joel 2).

Over and over the text paints us a picture of the Spirit: s/he looks like wind, fire, a dove, or clouds; s/he sounds like rushing wind or a still, small voice (Acts 2, etc.).

The Spirit embodies both genders. The terms for "spirit" in both Hebrew (*ruach*) and Greek (*pneuma*) are feminine nouns. It's believed that this feminine emphasis was done purposely so theology wouldn't be so dominated by masculine characteristics.

The gifts of the Spirit are either given or they're something we work really, really hard to attain. Weirdly, sometimes the Spirit is already present in people (for instance, Joshua in Numbers 27:15-20), and sometimes the Spirit comes to a person in a dramatic way.

So that should clear up any questions we had about the Spirit. Pneumatology, *check*.

It's no wonder the church doesn't have a theology of the Holy Spirit that everyone agrees with, let alone that youth ministry would be a place where we can wrestle with understanding such a mystery.

This is why I'm incredibly fond of the Celtic Christians' imagery for the Spirit. A dove like the one at Jesus' baptism is all well and good, but their experience of the Holy Spirit reminded them more of a wild goose. Doves are symbols of peace, purity, and shalom. They seem to show up in moments when all is right with the world: weddings, baptisms, celebrations—anything fancy and good. We use them to mark moments like this because of the wholeness and restoration they represent, but also because they are domesticated and fairly docile creatures that are unlikely to attack you.

I love the hope of the dove and all that she symbolizes; but the wild goose is closer to how I experience the presence and work of the Holy Spirit. Wild geese are untamed and unpredictable, and they're always going someplace. They can be loud, annoying—even scary. Geese will bite you if they feel trapped (even if you're only five years old and just trying to offer them a crust of bread after your mom said it was okay. I'm fine now. Really.)

The Holy Spirit isn't tame. We can't predict where or how s/he will show up. When it comes to God, we should expect the unexpected. We cannot capture the Spirit with our words, our rituals, or our good intentions.

The more I work with teenagers, the more I fall in love with the Holy Spirit. I don't mean love in the romantic comedy way, where we run toward each other in slow motion after many hilarious misunderstandings. I mean the sort of love that can develop only when you need each other, when it's a matter of life and death.

I can hold all the hope and love in the world for my students, but I can't make them love Jesus any more than I can make them do their homework or respect their parents. I can't force them to care about the kingdom. The only thing that does that is when the Spirit connects with their deepest desires.

Tuning in to the Holy Spirit is incredibly good news to youth workers because we can begin to see ourselves as co-creators with God in our ministry. It's not up to us. Our task is to be faithfully present to our students and to the movement of the Holy Spirit. We get to participate in making more goodness, more beauty, more love, more of the kingdom of God as we pay attention to what the Spirit is doing in our midst.

Ministry that ignores the Spirit can make us frantic, crazy people who think it's all up to us. Have you ever had a conversation with someone where you're pretty sure the other person already knows what he or she wants to say to you, regardless of what you're saying? Now compare that experience to a conversation where your friend listened and responded to what you were actually saying. When we forget the Holy Spirit's ability to speak to us and to our students, we are like well-intentioned bulldozers with an agenda, running amuck through others' dignity and desires. Our best work is to be present and respond as the Spirit's co-con*spirit*ors. (Ha. Get it?)

A robust theology of the Holy Spirit invites us to humility and the delicious risk of helplessness that comes with holding our plans and agendas loosely. It's scary at first. But relinquishing our perceived control over the spiritual well-being of our students and their families frees us to actually love and pastor them faithfully. The Spirit allows us to let go of whatever pressure we feel to change students or save students, so we may simply *be with* our students as we all attend to the presence of God in our midst. This is what pastors do.

If God's Spirit is present like a wild goose, then forming adolescents according to their good desires is an unpredictable process. It's never clear to us exactly what will happen, and it requires a lot of trust to believe God can be present in so much wildness. But God does some of God's best work in the wild.

Adolescence is a wild goose chase. Rather than being the most underrated person of the Trinity, the Holy Spirit might ring truest for people during the teenage years. Teens might find something of themselves reflected in the wildness, unpredictability, and adventure of the wild goose. They might be compelled by the idea that God shows up all the time and in ways we'd never expect. Remember how their brains crave new stimuli? Enter the capricious Holy Spirit.

The Spirit is present always and everywhere, working in everything good, true, beautiful, loving, and living to reconcile all things to God. S/he reveals where God is already present and comforts us in the broken places where the kingdom is not yet a full reality.

Our students might be our greatest teachers when it comes to being open to the movement of the Spirit.

I once had a group of sixth grade boys who were obsessed with Kirby, the pink marshmallow-looking video game character. They found a way to steer just about every conversation we had into Kirby-land, making most of the girls roll their eyes. I tried playing it cool, asking them questions about why they loved Kirby so much and encouraging them to talk about it after youth group ended.

One day we were talking about how the Holy Spirit shows up in our lives and maybe gives us gifts like kindness and patience. Right on cue, Luke got this mischievous grin on his face and said something ridiculous about Kirby, careening the conversation off course.

I guess I was feeling braver than usual because I decided to bite instead of redirect: "What about the Holy Spirit made you think about Kirby, Luke?" To my shame, I fully expected him to give up and be quiet.

Luke thought about it for a second. "Well, Kirby goes around inhaling bad guys, and he absorbs their powers at different parts of each level. So maybe the Holy Spirit does that. Maybe the Holy Spirit helps us have what we need at different parts of life."

I'm not sure how I responded. I hope I was wise enough to just be quiet or thank him for revealing the Spirit in a way that I never would have thought possible.

Remember Jacob? He woke up and said, "Surely the Lord is in this place—and I did not know it!" (Genesis 28:16). That's me. That's us. Every time we give students space to wonder what the Holy Spirit is up to.

The most significant moments of our becoming are rarely accomplished through logical systems or premeditated formulas. While these have value and can be incredibly meaningful, the transformation of a person requires something less tangible, something that can barely be put into words. There is no telling what—whether it's extraordinary or mundane—will awaken us to joy, goodness, awe, hope, or a deep sense of shalom.

We need to offer students a faith that can embrace these transcendent moments where we suspect there is much more going on around us than we first realized. For students it could be a perfect song coming on the radio, driving with the windows down, snapping a photo, or a good talk with a friend.

If we truly believe "the earth is the Lord's and all that is in it" (Psalm 24:1) and there is no place we can flee from God's presence (Psalm 139), then we must offer students an understanding of God here and now. Our work is to continue becoming the sort of people and pastors that awaken, like Jacob, to God's presence in places we didn't previously expect.

Whenever we become aware of the Spirit, we become more the person we were created to be. Our identity is formed over time by thousands of moments that could be either holy or mundane. The difference between sacred and secular is *us*, and whether we will choose to bless or curse.

We hope students will begin to see that God is always present and that in the Christian life we are called to recognize that presence as the deepest reality. If the whole earth is full of God's presence, then truth is all over the place and we can be a part of it. Rob Bell writes:

> The point of our stories and our faith journeys is that they are about something much bigger. . . . All things are yours. Being a Christian is not cutting yourself off from real life; it is entering into it more fully. It is not failing to go deeper; it is going deeper than ever. It is a journey into the heart of how things really are. What is it that makes you feel alive? What is it that makes your soul soar?[15]

Students long to experience God within their lives, and sometimes they only need permission to name their transcendent moments as God-saturated. Students have other places for socializing, studying, and recreating; but rarely are they given the opportunity to be themselves in the presence of God with a community who loves them.

What if all middle school boys thought of the Holy Spirit when they were playing video games? Can you imagine how that would form them into a certain sort of person who is tuned in to God's presence in the rest of their lives? There is nothing too humble or irrelevant for God to touch.

God assigns holiness to ordinary, earthy things all the time:

Are you a descendant of Abraham? Cut your penis to show that you are set apart as God's.

Did you witness something miraculous? Set up a pile of rocks so that when you come back to this place, you will remember what God has done.

Remember how God saved you from slavery? Eat unleavened bread and bitter herbs.

Need to be made ritually pure? Bathe in water.

Isn't this the point of Communion? Jesus took common cornerstones of a meal, bread and wine, and made them a holy reminder of his life, death, resurrection, and ascension. For the rest of their lives, whenever the disciples broke bread or drank wine, they were vividly reminded of Jesus.

"Remember?" the Spirit whispers in ordinary things, "Remember how you saw God, and God loved you?"

Anything that reveals something of God's presence is a sacrament.

The Spirit goes everywhere, if only we'd attune our senses to see, hear, touch, smell, and taste the presence of God all around us.

The same ancient Celtic Christians that came up with the wild goose imagery had revolutionary ideas about evangelism. Rather than believing they had to take the gospel to other places where God was not present, they believed the Holy Spirit was already at work ahead of them. They understood that God's presence wasn't bound to a specific manifestation: it might look, feel, taste, sound, and smell different in other places than what they were familiar with. Wherever they went, they expected to encounter the wild goose Spirit that is always moving.

There is no place that God's presence is not.
The wild goose is on the move, here and now, wherever and whenever we are.

There is no difference between the secular and the spiritual worlds, except our perception. Consider Paul's words to the Galatians about life in the Spirit and the fruit of the Spirit:

> Live by the Spirit, I say, and do not gratify the desires of the flesh. For what the flesh desires is opposed to the Spirit, and what the Spirit desires is opposed to the flesh; for these are opposed to each other, to prevent you from doing what you want. But if you are led by the Spirit, you are not subject to the law. Now the works of the flesh are obvious: fornication, impurity, licentiousness, idolatry, sorcery, enmities, strife, jealousy, anger, quarrels, dissensions, factions, envy, drunkenness, carousing, and things like these. I am warning you, as I warned you before: those who do such things will not inherit the kingdom of God.
>
> By contrast, the fruit of the Spirit is love, joy, peace, patience, kindness, generosity, faithfulness, gentleness, and self-control. There is no law against such things. And those who belong to Christ Jesus have crucified the flesh with its passions and desires. If we live by the Spirit, let us also be guided by the Spirit. (Galatians 5:16–25)

Paul warns them about "the desires of the flesh," a phrase that has given all desire a bad, undeserved rap. Paul isn't saying all desire is evil; he's speaking about what happens when good desires get twisted and broken. He juxtaposes these fleshy desires with what we desire when we're aligned with the Spirit.

I think Paul must have made those lists because he knew how easy it is to mistake the shoddy knockoff for the real thing. It's easy to mistake sex for love, idols for God, hatred for justice, and ambition for joy. Paul's language is so strong that I think, just to be safe, we've written off the whole category of desire and do everything we can to grow the fruit of the Spirit without it. It doesn't help that we tend to read "will not inherit the kingdom of God" (v. 21) as "will go straight to hell." I think Paul means what he says: those who insist on pursuing misdirected desires will not encounter the kingdom of heaven on earth; they won't find the gospel to be good news here and now.

When I was a teenager and we learned about the fruit of the Spirit in youth group, we spent a week on each attribute. It was presented as though we could develop love one week, peace another, and so on until week nine when we would be a perfect Spirit fruit basket, devoid of any desires that might be too fleshy. The fear of hell was always a good motivator to become perfect quickly.

What if Paul intended to communicate that wherever we see love, joy, peace, patience, kindness, goodness, faithfulness, gentleness and self-control—that's where the Spirit is moving? What if when Paul asks us to "be guided by the Spirit" (v. 25), he meant we'd find life in *everything* that reflected the presence of God?

Something of God's presence is in everything loving, joyful, peaceful, patient, kind, good, faithful, gentle, and disciplined. And the Spirit is grieved when these things find their expression in broken, misguided actions.

Our theology doesn't always match our practice. Most Christians believe God is omnipresent; it's a fairly orthodox tradition. Yet we are more surprised when we encounter the

Spirit than when we don't.

It seems like our default is to assume that God is absent unless we click our heels three times, do our devotionals, sing our favorite songs, go to church, or have a certain emotional experience. How many of our students are afflicted with spiritual trauma from retreats and mission trips because they have a profound encounter with God and then go home to a feeling that God is absent? Yet the Spirit is already there, waiting for us.

It's no coincidence that Hebrews used the same word for "wind," "breath," and "spirit": *ruach*. Whatever life throws at us, whether we feel close to God or far away, our breath connects us to the ever-present Spirit. We don't even have to think about it or articulate it.

Breathe in, God is within us.
Breathe out, God surrounds us.

Even in the depths of despair, Job vowed to be faithful to God for "as long as my breath is in me and the spirit of God is in my nostrils" (Job 27:3). Wherever there is breath, there is life, there is the Spirit. Our breathing is blessed.

I'm not asking you to take up yoga. Just consider what it would do to your life and your relationship with God if you paused a few times a day to notice your breathing and remember that the Spirit is within you and all around you.

When you're heartbroken and when you're winning,
whether you're lonely or sought,
if you're living a comedy or a tragedy,
God is with you.

This is the tension of the Spirit's work: s/he reveals where the kingdom already is and comforts us where the kingdom is not yet fully realized.

Jesus told the disciples that the Spirit would remind them of everything Jesus had said (John 14:26). I truly believe that one of God's great kindnesses to humanity is that God knows we forget. The Spirit is present at all times to remind us of who Jesus is and everything he said about the way of the kingdom.

When did you last catch a glimpse of heaven on earth? Aren't these the things that keep us going? We crave things that remind us that all is not lost, that our faith in humanity can be restored. The Spirit reveals these things so that instead of assuming something is just a random act of kindness, we might see the kingdom of God breaking through.

I do all of my writing at a magical café called Chocolati that's just a short walk from my apartment. In the cozy glow of a table lamp, I sit and sip chai lattes by day and merlot by night. I also eat the occasional sea salt vanilla dark chocolate truffle because this place makes treats that taste like unicorn vitamins.

But for me, the baristas are the best part of the experience. They've slowly come to understand why I stalk them at work. We've learned each others' names and a bit of the stories that bring us to this enchanted caffeine dispensary.

One day when I came in, my dear friend the barista flapped something at me from behind the espresso machine. Confused, I took it from her. It was a cloth for cleaning a computer screen, and there was a note taped to it: BELONGS TO MORGAN (THE PASTOR). Delighted, I laughed and explained the cloth wasn't even mine, but I thanked her for thinking it might be. It had been found at my favorite table, so the baristas wanted to be sure they returned it to me.

Maybe this exchange wouldn't make a *normal* person giddy, but it made my day.

The kingdom of God is already here, and it's like being named and recognized by new friends.

On another night, my husband Ian came to the café to sit with me. He recognized that perhaps the bags under my eyes didn't jive with my thoughts on how youth pastors are human beings and not productive machines. Gently, he closed my laptop and said, "Just go for a walk, Morgan. Walk around the block and see what happens."

As it turns out, just a block from my café—in the middle of a quiet residential neighborhood—there is a little Buddhist monastery! Outside they have a beautiful circle of prayer wheels, worn metal cylinders that you spin as you walk around and meditate. Prayer flags sway gently overhead, whispering prayers to the wind even when no one is looking. I walked slowly, savoring the cool metal against my fingers and murmuring a sophisticated theological prayer:

Hello?
Help?
Peace?
Please?
Thank you?

It's not quite how Jesus taught the disciples to pray, but I think he gets it.

The Spirit reminds us that kingdom of heaven is already here, and it's like finding a sanctuary around the block.

The Spirit meets us in our desires—even the ones we don't know we have—and s/he shows us how redeemed the world already is. We can taste and see that God is good, here and now. Our good desires act like a compass, always orienting us to the reality of the kingdom.

The world is always tipping toward redemption.

Yet our hope is brokenhearted. We are made for wholeness, for our good desires to be fulfilled in extravagance and generosity. Our deepest spirit remembers that we were created to live in paradise. We are no strangers to pain, loss, and death.

My great-grandmother passed away a few years ago. As the "spiritual" one in our family, I was asked to offer her eulogy. It was the first time I'd ever presided at a funeral, and I was at a loss. I scoured my Bible trying to find something comforting to say, but I kept coming up empty. I jotted down a few halfhearted, defeated notes and prayed God would make meaning of them somehow.

Most of what I did at that podium was weep. I think that's one of the most kingdom-y, gospel-y things Jesus did when facing the death of a loved one. The weird, wonderful thing about Jesus weeping for Lazarus was that Jesus was fully aware that death doesn't have the last word. He must have already had the idea of bringing Lazarus back, and he understood better than anyone that one day resurrection will be for everyone (John 11).

But he wept. Because no amount of hope or assurance makes death any less painful.

Death is not okay; it's not right. We weren't made to die, but to *live*. And we feel that deep within us. When we are stuck between the already and the not-yet kingdom, the Spirit is with us to remind us and comfort us with the hope that God still brings life from death. It's a mystery how it all works, but it's a promise we cling to as we follow in the way of Jesus.

Perhaps today we'll be surprised by the Spirit turning darkness to light. Maybe it's happening a lot more often than we know, and we keep trying to be formed into the sort of people who can see it.

Maybe the world stays broken today. Despite our prayers and our faith, perhaps our miracle never comes. When we don't know what to pray, the Spirit intercedes on our behalf with wordless groans that mirror our grief (Romans 8:26). Jesus called the Spirit our Comforter and our Advocate (John 14:16), present with us when it's clear the kingdom isn't here yet.

During the process of writing this book, our sweet golden retriever, Toby, went to be Jesus' dog. This initiated us into a sacred club for those who've experienced the loss of a beloved pet, a lot of people who just happened to share life with the best animal in the world. It's the worst. Nothing can make it okay.

Yet I found my broken heart showered with comfort and beauty. Sorrow and love flow mingled down.[16]

As Toby got worse and Ian and I started wrestling with making an unthinkable choice, a friend put us in touch with his veterinarian, Lisa, who lives in another state. Sight unseen, Lisa walked us through Toby's final days. She texted me and took my sobbing phone calls, answering all of my desperate questions day and night. Ultimately, she assured us we were doing the right thing, that this would be our final act of love for Toby.

The Spirit comforts us that the kingdom of heaven is here, like one who comforts us when we grieve.

One day there will be no more tears.

Toby had the entire neighborhood wrapped around his paw. He loved to make the rounds, two blocks up and two blocks back, which conveniently took us to all four of the local establishments that offer dog treats and attention. Our bank was his favorite, if you can believe it. Whether we had banking to do or not, they lavished him with love and would send him skidding across the tile floor after a tennis ball.

On his last day, the bank was our final stop between the beach and his bed. "Toby's Best Day," we called it. From the tellers to the manager, they all came out to the car by turn, bringing treats for Toby and weeping with us.

Afterward, I stayed away for a week. I felt undone and unable to walk our familiar route. Then one day I picked up the mail and found a hand-addressed package from our bank. Everyone had signed a sympathy card and chipped in to buy us a book about how great golden retrievers are.

The Spirit comforts us that the kingdom of God is here, like a neighborhood who loved an old dog.

One day everything will be new.

Remember, beloved, that death does not have the final word. Even our mourning is part of our salvation.

The Spirit reminds us that there is goodness in the world, though it comes hand-in-hand with loss. S/he reminds us that the kingdom is already breaking through our brokenness. The things we desire are already here: love, peace, comfort, beauty, justice, and wholeness. As we pay attention to our good desire, we see more and more how often the Spirit insists that all is not lost after all—or if it is, it's lost for only a little while. Christians have a choice. We can view these experiences as mere coincidences—something nice that happened once—or revelations of heaven on earth. As our souls awaken to the Spirit who is always present, we begin to see how cheap the word *coincidence* can be. God is on the move. The Spirit shows us how the kingdom is already here, love is real, and our desires might not be unrequited after all.

This is a leap of faith, to be sure. There are so many moments when I believe it's far more likely that God is taking a nap and hitting the snooze button instead of being dynamically present. . As a rule, I think Christians find it much easier to believe evil's ability to wreck everything than the Spirit's ability to make us whole.

Ever wonder why a song, book, or movie becomes especially popular? Usually it's because the creator tapped into this universal work of the Spirit and revealed that goodness is here and more goodness is yet to come, despite our many losses. These stories tap into our desire to participate in saving the world. Maybe this is part of becoming like little children in our faith, because kids have an insatiable desire for justice and happy endings.

As the Spirit encourages us by showing how the world is already being saved and comforting us in brokenness, s/he also works with us to embody the gospel here and now as our ever-present collaborator.

The Spirit teaches us how to participate with God in the restoration of all things; maybe the more common term for this would be *mission*. It's not like a mission of military precision in which we're assigned a particular limb of the body of Christ where we remain, whether we like it or not. But it's a mission which connects our unique desires to the work of the Spirit to keep wooing creation back to the Creator.

When we speak about mission, living in sync with the work of God in the world, we reach the other end of the Spirit's spectrum of influence. S/he is everywhere and yet profoundly located in specific times and places too. The invitation of the Christian life, and the point of all discipleship and formation, is to join in with what God is doing wherever we find ourselves.

This is the Spirit of *Emmanuel*, which means "God with us." The Israelites called God's presence the *Shekinah*, which means "to inhabit or dwell," as if these followers of Yahweh understood that God was their neighbor first and foremost.

We are learning to orient our lives around the gospel question. What is good news for him or her, right here, right now?

How does their desire for goodness, wholeness, beauty, truth, justice, and life connect us in this very moment to God's heart for the world and the work of the Holy Spirit to redeem?

Can you imagine what might happen if you asked the teenagers in your neighborhood or town or city what they really want? What if our ministries scratched where teenagers actually itch? What if we figured out a way to collaborate with God in revealing students' great victories and comforting students' broken hearts?

The best qualitative question I've ever been asked in an attempt to assess my ministry was this: "If your ministry vanished from your neighborhood, would the community be heartbroken?"

As we seek to form students by connecting their good desires to what God is doing, the Spirit is our ever-present Advocate, Comforter, and Collaborator. S/he goes everywhere, reveals the kingdom, comforts us in our brokenness, and works with us to restore the world. Our best work is to pay attention, listen to the Spirit, and join in—while inviting our students to do the same.

9

FOLLOW THE STUDENT

Who is youth ministry for?

I really want the answer to be students, and sometimes it is. But most youth ministry is for adults.

It's complicated since youth pastors are accountable to the whole church. Often the vision and trajectory of our community is out of our hands, and we're asked to come alongside and offer support through the youth program. Some of us make a living at this, so the relationship between being a member of a faith community and being an employee of that community gets messy sometimes. We all have to pay our rent, and that can mean we don't get to do what we dream about when it comes to the students in our care.

Everybody wants something different. Again, it all boils down to desire. So we have to work from there. Parents are looking for a program; they want a particular place and time where their teenagers will be safe, have fun, and learn how to be good Christians. This is where youth ministry gets its reputation for being somewhat tunnel-visioned about equating discipleship with faith-based morality and dodgeball. For most of us, one of our main (although rarely articulated) responsibilities is to keep parents happy.

Don't get me wrong, parents are still the most important influence on a student's formation. Youth workers should consider it a privilege to come alongside parents and support them. However, parents also tend to remember youth group as a glorious retrospective and want their kids to have the same glowing experience. Most forget how they put their own faith on the backburner until they had kids because they didn't see any point in finding a church when they went to college, or joined the Peace Corps, or started their careers. Alternatively, many parents think the point of youth group is to keep their kid safe, happy, entertained, morally upright, and sex-free. Also, they tithe (i.e., they pay our salaries). So it can sometimes feel like we have 30 or even 100 bosses with unarticulated expectations looking over our shoulders, even though we're all supposed to be on the same team.

"I'd love for youth group to be a place where my child tunes in to her desires and becomes more of a whole person as she learns what it means to follow in the way of Jesus and participate in bringing the kingdom of God to earth," said no parent ever.

Except I think most parents would really love it if this were true. Few of us have seen this sort of discipleship in action, so we can't even imagine how good it could be. I think students are more intrigued by this than they are by being entertained and indoctrinated. That's what the rest of the world offers them, but there is no loving place for them to explore their souls.

Forming students according to their desires means we respond to what they want in the context of our ministries, even if they don't fully know how to articulate what they're looking for just yet. There are a lot of categories for talking about adolescent desire in general, but three in particular stand out as being fairly universal to the teenage experience: someone to become, somewhere to belong, and something to do. (We'll go more in-depth about these desires in the next three chapters.)

The best thing anyone ever said to me about the way I pastor students absolutely broke my heart. A dear friend had just started volunteering with our middle schoolers. After her first couple of Sundays, I asked how she was doing and what she thought of being a part of our ministry.

She said, "I really like that we treat them like people."

She went on to tell me that based on her experience and what she knew about youth ministry, kids were funneled through a program, given the prescribed teachings, entertained, and then sent on their way as well-trained religious consumers.

My ego wants to believe I've tapped into some mysterious youth ministry magic, like this valuing of human desire is some profound way of being that no one else knows about—similar to how I invented the concept of making s'mores with Reese's Peanut Butter Cups. (I wish.)

There is nothing new under the sun, just new arrangements of deep old things. This is not some sort of Gnostic secret wisdom that only the enlightened can attain. It's for everybody because everybody already knows how to do it. We just need to give ourselves permission and then practice a bit.

We get so bogged down in everything that youth ministry is *supposed* to be, that we forget it's as simple as treating teenagers like good human beings and reminding them that God thinks they're good human beings too.

The other word for this is *love*.

We love students or else we wouldn't do this work.

Loving them is how we participate in bringing more of the kingdom of heaven to earth.

It's worship.

And worship is how we express the way our desires connect to God.

Every good desire is an invitation to worship.

As youth pastors, we can't hope to share or understand the diversity of desires our students bring. What they're looking for and what we're looking for, in life and in faith, are probably really different. But all desires have the potential to draw us to the One who desired all of this in the first place. Our stories are all different, and hearing about what is sacred to teenagers only encourages us in our own spiritual journeys.

After all, we're not trying to make teenagers into mini clones of Jesus; we're trying to help them figure out how to follow Jesus in their own way.

There's plenty of holiness to go around.

Treating students like people means we invite their whole selves—all of their desires, both broken and beautiful—into conversation with their faith. They don't have to check any part of themselves at the door, or hide who they are to fit some Christian image. Spiritual formation at its best is collaboration, learning from one another's experience and perspective to gain a fuller picture of who we are and who God is. We weren't made to figure it all out alone.

A starting question for students to consider might be, "What do you want from youth group?"

The ministry is for them, after all. We're all wasting our time if they're not interested in what's going on. They may not be able to articulate what they want; but by asking the question, we invite them to start participating in their own spiritual formation.

Whenever you start working at a new church, the sage wisdom you'll hear is not to make any changes in your first year. Or if you do, go molasses-slow. I've been at St. Andrew's for a year now, and I've been making changes painfully slowly. The high school youth ministry I inherited from my predecessor was built almost exclusively on community: kids sharing about their lives and having a place where they could say whatever was on their minds. It has been a really meaningful place for many of them. A few months in, it became clear that it was pretty abnormal to go any deeper than a weekly update about their various games, grades, and social lives. Talking about God seemed pretty much out of the question, like drinking poison or kicking puppies.

My co-leader, Danny, and I spent the better part of a year listening to their stories and responding with questions to get to know them better. Danny is brilliant. He's a therapist who has an amazing ability to engage students on an emotional level and read group dynamics. I am always learning from him, and we really complement each other as leaders, besides being dear friends. Everyone needs a Danny.

Together we created some opportunities to integrate deeper conversations into our summer mission trip. We asked some open-ended questions and made it clear that we weren't looking for any "right" or religious answers, just their honest responses. We acknowledged that it wasn't the norm for the group to talk about God, and we asked them if it would be all right to play with the conversation, no pressure. If they weren't comfortable, they could change the subject to something else they really cared about.

Given the space to wonder about their souls, our students really opened up. It was an honor to sit with them and try to express where we saw God, where we didn't, and where we wished God would show up in our lives.

The amazing thing? These students who once seemed allergic to religious dialogue of any kind suddenly came alive. When we returned to our regular gathering back home, we asked if there was anything from the trip that they'd like to keep doing throughout the rest of the year.

"Maybe we could have some more deep conversations about stuff. That was pretty cool."

They want good things.
They are thirsty for good news.
They love being invited to participate.
I am honored to follow as they lead me into the realm of their desires.

Forming students according to what they actually care about means we treat them like the good, desiring human beings they are. Treating teenagers like people is the defining mark of great youth ministry.

Much has been said about *relational ministry*, and I'd be willing to bet that's a term most of us use to describe the way we minister to students. This particular philosophy is the subject of countless books, university courses, blogs, and conference sessions. It's one of our favorite buzzwords. And usually what we mean by *relational* is that we structure programs so adult leaders are invested in the lives of students in a particular way.

However, even the most relational ministries can host content—through the curriculum, talks, and conversations—that degrades into coercive programs that take us far away from our relational intentions because they're driven by a particular agenda. We come with a plan of what we want students to learn or become, squeezing their lives into the mold of our message. This is the edge of spiritual manipulation and abuse, a trap that's easy to fall into if we believe we have a monopoly on what the Christian life should look like.

Our well-intentioned, practiced teachings often serve as a way of limiting our students' ability to participate in an authentic way with themselves, the rest of the community, and God. Much of mainstream Christian theology has difficulty holding space for people to be broken, to struggle, to doubt without being silenced by shallow Christian truisms:

Do you doubt God? Just have faith.
Are you struggling with something in your life? You should pray about it.
Did you accomplish something amazing? Praise the Lord! God really worked through you even though you're a slimy sinner.
Do you ever wonder about your sexuality? Nope. Stop it. Also, no purple.
How should you relate to the world? Love the sinner, hate the sin.

We offer relationships, but only on the church's terms. It's like we're all playing a game called "Let's Pretend." It's based on us pretending that:

You are not what you are.
What we're teaching makes a difference in your lives.

167

What bores you is important, and that the more you are bored, the more important it is.
There are certain things that every Christian must believe.
Both the questions and answers about the Christian faith have been fixed for all time.
Your spirituality and eternal destination can be judged on the basis of how well you play Let's Pretend.[17]

No healthy relationship asks us to pretend in order to participate.

It wouldn't go too well if I told my friends or my husband or my boss exactly what to care about or how to behave in our relationship so they could avoid shame and eternal damnation.

True relational ministry invites students to bring their whole selves and their unique voices to bear on the ministry we create together. They have desires and a trajectory all their own—ones we could never claim to be an authority of because we aren't them. Orienting our ministries around desire means we give students' personhood more weight than we give our own ministry schemes because our ultimate plan is that they will become more and more the men and women God made them to be.

This is more attractive to them than any particular program, game, video, or message we can imagine. Adolescents have so few places where they are given ownership of their own becoming. It's rare for them to speak their minds and have it count. Teenagers are basically told what to do, who to become, and what they should want from dawn until dusk: home, school, extracurriculars, homework. Few places are fully their own, where an adult who cares about them will give them space to flex their being, take up space, and practice who they are becoming in a way that is loving, supportive, and safe.

Youth ministries that value desire look much more like a sailboat than a cruise ship. A cruise is a finely tuned entertainment machine, with consumption being the only participation that's expected of the passengers. Ministries that offer a menu of prefabricated programs and curricula in an all-inclusive package miss the particularity and diversity of students' desires. And they fail to form teenagers' faith in a sustainable way because those desires don't get connected to God in ways that are meaningful to each student.

A sailboat, on the other hand, requires the participation of everyone in the crew. Everybody has a different part to play in order to move in the same direction—toward adventure, fun, or whatever awaits. This is what ministry is like when we invite our students to collaborate with us, responding to the movement of the Spirit-wind toward the realization of the kingdom. We all do our part, it's hard work, and sometimes we have to zigzag our way to our destination.

Pastoring a crew is hard. It means we don't have our hand on every control, ropes sometimes get tangled, and we get off course from time to time. Yet we have faith that the Spirit is always with us, breathing wind into our journey. We are wonderfully, helplessly dependent on the movement of the Spirit. Sort of like life.

Our role is to be faithfully present as we follow our students' desires and keep helping them make connections between life and God. This means giving up our obsession with results and with reaching a predetermined destination in order to focus on what is right before us.

We must always respond to where our students are, not where we *wish* they were, and be willing to change our plans accordingly. It's silly to continue with an agenda or a lesson that no one cares about. Without investment, without making some connection to their hearts' desires, our words will go in one ear and out the other—most likely sparking some feelings of boredom and annoyance in between. As we practice, and the better we truly know our students, the better we'll be at facilitating the sort of content that flexes with the needs and attentions of our audience.

As Neil Postman and Charles Weingartner wrote in *Teaching as a Subversive Activity*:

> The only kind of lesson plan, or syllabus, that makes sense to [the student] is one that tries to predict, account for, and deal with the authentic responses of learners to a particular problem: the kinds of questions they will ask, the obstacles they will face, their attitudes, and the possible solutions they will offer, etc.[18]

It's brave to change course when students' eyes glaze over. Going off script, straying from our notes, or scrapping our big idea can be terrifying. The most important part of communication is whether the other person connects to what you said. If he doesn't, then it's all just good intentions.

When I was first practicing this, it was occasionally disastrous. Sometimes my team and I would stumble out into the sunlight after church, shaking our heads and wondering if this flexibility was worth it. Following teenagers' desires sometimes meant we had to lovingly and patiently sift through a lot of distractions in order to understand what they thought was good, loving, true, or life-giving.

It wasn't pretty, but it was beautiful.

One day we were talking about Moses, the burning bush, and how sometimes God shows up in unexpected ways. They were being kind and polite, I could tell, but their hearts weren't connecting. As I invited them to respond to the story, to ask questions and wonder together, we spun off into a different universe entirely.

"What about angels?"

What?

"What about angels? Why aren't there angels anymore?" Sleepy eyes popped open, suddenly interested.

It is beyond me what triggered them to think about angels when we were talking about Moses. Maybe it was the fire or the weird heavenly voice, I have no idea. But I set my Moses notes aside and started to ask questions.

What made you think about angels?
Have you ever seen or heard an angel?
What do you think they're like? What's their job?
What do angels tell you about who God is?

Amazing things happened when we started following our students' lead. Our students got to help create the conversation each week with their questions, ideas, and creativity. We got to tell stories about our lives and show our love by paying attention to each other. My team and I didn't teach so much as we facilitated dialogue, sharing what we knew to be true alongside the wisdom of middle school students.

What we say doesn't matter unless it matters to them.

I know that sucks. We work so hard to bring some quality content to our programs. But we can't love the *idea* of teaching more than teaching itself.

To speak of the meaning that students make from our ministries is vulnerable and brave. It means looking beyond our intentions to what students actually receive from their experience. It means giving up control and adopting a posture of humility in order to be more faithfully present.

Formation and discipleship in our various ministries fit along a spectrum from dead serious to laissez faire. We find ourselves swinging on a pendulum. On one side there's a particular articulated understanding of what Christian discipleship looks like; on the other side we throw our spiritual hands in the air like we just don't care, so long as everyone is having a good time and feeling connected.

Somewhere in the middle is the sweet spot where youth ministry is improvisation.

Tina Fey has four rules for making improv awesome:

Rule #1: Agree
The first rule of improvisation is AGREE. Always agree and SAY YES. When you're improvising, this means you are required to agree with whatever your partner has created. So if we're improvising and I say, "Freeze, I have a gun!" and you say, "That's not a gun. It's your finger. You're pointing your finger at me," our improvised scene has ground to a halt. But if I say, "Freeze, I have a gun!" and you say, "The gun I gave you for Christmas! You bastard!" then we have started a scene because we have AGREED that my finger is in fact a Christmas gun.

Rule #2: Say Yes, And
The second rule of improvisation is not only to say yes, but YES, AND. You are supposed to agree and then *add something of your own*. If I start a scene with "I can't believe it's so hot in here," and you just say, "Yeah . . ."

we're kind of at a standstill. But if I say, "I can't believe it's so hot in here," and you say, "What did you expect? We're in hell . . . " now we're getting somewhere.

Rule #3: Make Statements

This is a positive way of saying "Don't ask questions all the time." If we're in a scene and I say, "Who are you? Where are we? What are we doing here? What's in that box?" I'm putting pressure on you to come up with all the answers. . . . We've all worked with that person. That person is a drag. It's usually the same person around the office who says things like, "There's no calories in it if you eat it standing up!"

Rule #4: There Are No Mistakes . . . Only Opportunities

If I start a scene as what I think is very clearly a cop riding a bicycle, but you think I am a hamster in a hamster wheel, guess what? Now I'm a hamster in a hamster wheel. I'm not going to stop everything to explain that it was really supposed to be a bike. Who knows? Maybe I'll end up being a police hamster who's been put on a "hamster wheel" duty because I'm "too much of a loose cannon" in the field. In improv there are no mistakes, only beautiful happy accidents. And many of the world's greatest discoveries have been by accident. I mean, look at the Reese's Peanut Butter Cup, or Botox.[19]

What if we could approach spiritual formation and education in a way that was playful like this? These rules invite us to create space for students to encounter God on their own terms, without putting our own biases and baggage on them. We are most meaningfully formed when we encounter another person with mutual respect, respond to the other person's story, and reciprocate with our own. It's a beautiful give-and-take that teaches us how to be good human beings and, through the lens of our desires, draws us to God.

We are still responsible for having a plan. The risk here is that the pendulum swings to the laissez faire extreme and we have students running amok. There is still plenty of space to have a plan and an intentional direction in which we're trying to move. "Where there is no vision, the people perish" (Proverbs 29:18a, KJV).

As risky as it is to take cues from our students' desires, it also allows for incredible freedom and a lot of fun. We get to play with concepts, questions, and directions that we never would have thought of or imagined they were interested in. Then we get to see how God shows up in the midst of this thing we're creating together.

We get to curate space for them to encounter God. Of course, they're still learning and aren't always sure what they want. So it's guaranteed to get messy sometimes.

For reassurance, I take a page out of Gamaliel's playbook. This guy was an elder of the Sanhedrin, a Pharisee, and an expert in Jewish law. Acts 22:3 says that before he was an apostle, Paul studied at Gamaliel's feet while he was growing up in Jerusalem. Early in the life of the church, Peter and the other apostles were being persecuted by the Sanhedrin for preaching the gospel. It seems that popular opinion amongst the council was to kill the message of Jesus by killing the apostles.

Luke recounts the wise words that Gamaliel spoke in their defense:

> "Fellow Israelites, consider carefully what you propose to do to these men. For some time ago Theudas rose up, claiming to be somebody, and a number of men, about four hundred, joined him; but he was killed, and all who

followed him were dispersed and disappeared. After him Judas the Galilean rose up at the time of the census and got people to follow him; he also perished, and all who followed him were scattered. So in the present case, I tell you, keep away from these men and let them alone; because if this plan or this undertaking is of human origin, it will fail; but if it is of God, you will not be able to overthrow them—in that case you may even be found fighting against God!" (Acts 5:35–39)

May we approach our students' desires with our hands open, ready to hold precious whatever they bring to share with us. Let us trust, like Gamaliel did, that if their desires are from God, then they will last.

When we're with students, we never know what's going to happen. There is often hilarity. And if we're lucky, we'll make something true and meaningful together. This is the messy beauty of allowing our desires to connect with our experience of God, because it means that in many ways, we're following our students' lead as we bless their whole selves.

10
WANTED: SOMEONE TO BECOME

What do teenagers want? Their desires are conveniently aligned with the main tasks of growing up, or else those tasks would never be completed. A huge part of the teenager's job description is to explore her identity and become more and more her unique self. That means teens are weaving the stories of their lives and learning how to tell the truth about who they are in ways that are most meaningful to them.

This process of becoming demands authenticity and craves reality. They want this more than they want to be entertained—even when all anecdotal evidence suggests otherwise!

They want to be their real selves and go through a hundred or a thousand different iterations to figure out what way of being, thinking, dressing, believing, or relating is most like them. This task is not finished during the teenage years. Today, the life stage of adolescence often extends into one's twenties and thirties. We are always being formed into who we are, but the task begins in earnest when we are in middle school and high school, so it deserves the special attention of the church.

Who are you?

What a cruel question for a teenager. Actually, it still sounds cruel to me sometimes, especially if the person asking that question adds that I can't answer with what I do for a living.

Who are you? Oh, you're a youth pastor? No, I mean, WHO are you?

Go away. If you have an answer in mind that you'd like me to say, then just tell me what it is so we can be done here. Please don't heap shame on everyone who wants to identify with the things they do that they care about.

Nonetheless, the question "Who are you?" is important. We are haunted by it, hounded by it, always trying to find an answer that will satisfy our desires for who we want to be.

It's so complicated.

"Who are you?" touches on our past, present, and future. It encompasses all of our desires: fulfilled, unrequited, and abandoned over the entire course of our whole lives. We can't help but carry our past in our present, along with our hopes and fears about the future, and all of these conspire to make us who we are. Any identity question has the potential to remind us where we've been wounded and where we ache for something different moving forward.

With so many factors at play, we are constantly reinventing ourselves, from the mundane to the profound.

During the course of writing this book, I've come to hate that which I once loved (R.I.P., Dr. Pepper), been confirmed into the Episcopal Church, lost some friends I'd hoped to keep, and resolved to stop eating anything that once had lips (it just seems like if you have lips, then you probably have feelings, too).

I am not who I once was.

Each day asks us to remember ourselves and reimagine who we want to be. The tricky bit is there's no way to know, quantitatively, whether you're doing it right, because there's really no "right." Only *you* can determine if you've succeeded in your work of becoming. It's a qualitative kind of success.

Are you becoming more alive or less?
Are you serving love or serving hatred?
Do you create dignity or shame for yourself and others?
Are you building heaven on earth or hell on earth?

No one wakes up and decides these things with any degree of immediate success. There is no *POOF!* for personhood. Becoming ourselves takes practice, and adolescence is especially a time when students experiment with who they want to be. We become ourselves over time, in places, through relationships.

Part of becoming ourselves is naming our experiences, both the heartbreaking and the uplifting. Developmentally speaking, this is a tough task for adolescents since they're more inclined to stay in the moment and avoid the pain and confusion that reflection can cause. Many students engage with life passively, and they'll even claim that's what they want: Life just happens to them. Considering their past reminds them that they are wounded, that everything hasn't been perfect, and they haven't escaped unscathed. This sort of introspection is tough for students because they're also in the process of differentiating themselves and distancing their identities from their families'. This is the season of life when parents and heroes start to fall off pedestals, and childhood memories are revisited with suspicion.

It's not too surprising, then, that many students aren't willing to stay in this uncomfortable space. Figuring out who you are is a tough, gradual process, and it's not at all glamorous. Once upon a time, young people became themselves based on what they did and who (or what) they loved over the course of many years.

But our culture has co-opted desire and called it a sale. People have become connections and followers, their relational connection established with the push of a button.

Today, our world offers instantaneous identification based on what we consume and how we connect through social media.

Our culture insists that we can easily identify ourselves based on what we buy and possess. Adolescents are able to change their identities in the blink of an eye across hundreds of social media platforms. They fracture themselves into a dozen different personas simultaneously, with very few immediate consequences and the promise of an electronic emotional connection and validation from other online personas. They are constantly tending their online images, carefully crafting their projected selves, and cultivating digital reputations that have very little to do with their daily lives in the analog world. Love and community, while sometimes healthily supplemented by online interaction, can be substituted for that rush of dopamine we get when we receive virtual attention from other users.

Teenagers will do things just so they have something to report to the Internet. It can be heartbreaking to see their interests and hobbies become "likes," while idealism and activism become "shares." I'm sorry, but likes and shares don't magically become clean water in Africa, nor do they make you a philanthropist. Recent studies have indicated that use of social media can actually depress us because the lives people project and the causes people support are so far removed from reality, it causes jealousy and generally crushes the human spirit. Having a thousand followers and very few friends is breaking us.

"Who am I?" can never be a question of instant gratification.

I am constantly wondering how we can help teenagers be less fractured and more whole, while at the same time understanding they have to experiment in order to become who they most wish to be. What if we could help them be present to themselves in the world around them with #NoFilter, instead of feeling like they must perform in order to meet a cultural standard of beauty and success, or a church standard of faithfulness and purity?

Adolescents' lives become compartmentalized and fractured when others' wishes and expectations overshadow their own emerging desires. Everybody wants something from them, and very few take the time to ask what a young person wants for himself.

We can't underestimate the role that desire plays in identity formation. If what we want most is an online persona, then more of our lives will revolve around keeping our digital doppelgängers thriving. Most students would do anything to protect and sustain the image they project into the world. Wherever we focus our energy becomes part of our identity.

We become what we want.

Don't take that imagery too far. You won't become a rainbow-vomiting unicorn or a mustachioed narwhal just because you want one.

Since our identities are rooted in emerging desires, they don't just *happen* to us. We are born unique people into unique situations, and then we're invited to participate in our own formation as human beings as we make choices along the way.

You don't just happen to you.

Following Jesus isn't inevitable for anyone. It's the result of a bunch of desires aligning to the point where it seems the best way to live is to love God. This is why when we seek to form students, we must pay attention to what they actually want. Our theology doesn't always allow space for the complexity of desire and identity that teenagers experience.

They could be sitting around the campfire on a retreat, singing with passion:

"Only you, Jesus, only you . . . "
"It's all about you, Jesus, and all this is for you . . . "
"All I need is you, Lord . . . "

And then they'll go meet up with the cute guy or girl from the next cabin over and make out.

But ALL they want is Jesus. Really. Really?

Desire is complicated, and pretending that it's not won't fool anybody.

In fact, teaching students to believe (pretend?) that all they want is Jesus can really stunt their identity formation because they don't get to explore what they *really* want and figure out how those things can connect to the Christian faith in a natural way. You want a boyfriend? Jesus is not your boyfriend. If you'd like to have a boyfriend, let's talk about how to do that in ways that are healthy and encourage you to keep becoming your good self.

We don't expect students to have themselves all figured out, but too often we expect them to be willing to make an eternal commitment of unwavering faith to an invisible God. It seems more realistic to expect their developmental uncertainty to work in tandem with spiritual faith and doubt.

Youth ministry oriented around desire will make it a priority to help students develop an authentic identity based on what they actually want in life. We can't replace their desires with Jesus, but we can help them connect their good desires to their experiences of God in a way that will help them sustain their faith over the course of their lives.

How can the church help students begin to answer this question of identity? By creating space for students to be themselves as they encounter God and others, and do it in such a way that no part of them feels unwelcome. Since identity isn't something we can just download into our students, it means inviting students to collaborate and participate in their own formation.

We are always being formed. The question is by what? And how? After the games end and the laughter settles down, how do we offer meaningful content to students in our care?

Most of the teaching we do in youth ministry today is dialectic, meaning we speak, they listen, and we hope students learn something true. You know you're a dialectic teacher if:

You know exactly what students should learn from your talk.

If they learn it, they will instantly be changed or have a homework takeaway.

Your talk contains distinct categories of right and wrong, or a specific moral agenda.

You speak until you're done, without responding to your audience along the way.

You are the only one speaking.

You talk a lot about God in an abstract, distanced way.

This sort of teaching can be done very well, and it's a great way to interact with adults who already have a sense of self and the ability to think abstractly or critically about the concepts that others propose. This style of teaching is mostly not ideal for forming young people. It can be reminiscent of school lectures. It doesn't invite students to engage in the material on their own terms, but rather in whatever way the voice of authority deems appropriate. Teenagers will likely tune out, rebel, or accept everything the teacher says without question. None of these responses is very helpful in cultivating students' desire or constructing a healthy sense of self.

Many youth workers teach this way because it's been the go-to method of the church, and it's the way we were raised or trained. I remember learning as an undergrad about the specific formulas for speaking to youth that were most effective:

> Come in with a Big Idea.
> Use Hook, Book, Look, Took.
> Then they will love Jesus.
> (And sometimes they do.)

I just wonder if we can be more effective at inviting students' whole selves to play when we teach.

There is space for us to be much more creative in our teaching, as we help students figure out who they are and how their desires connect them to Jesus. The alternative to dialectic teaching is dialogue and conversation. This method was given a nod in my youth ministry classes as "emerging" teaching—there was a sense that this is something done by crazy, irresponsible youth workers who don't care about teenagers' souls, so go back to the dialectic and make sure they learn what they need to learn in order to stay out of hell. As I've served actual students, however, I've been more and more drawn to a dialogical approach.

Dialogic teaching is all about the process. It assumes that formation happens over time, that we are saved cumulatively rather than all at once. Since our desires change, we change; and since we change, our faith changes. The truth is that the content of our teaching will have as many different meanings as we have listeners, and so the very structure of our talk can reflect that anticipation. This doesn't mean there isn't substance to what we teach. Dialogic teaching is dripping with purpose, and, generally speaking, that purpose is to draw students to the kingdom of God and encourage them to follow in the way of Jesus. Everything connects back to this vision because the gospel can be reflected in anything good, loving, true, beautiful, or living.

You might be a dialogic teacher if:

You expect God to be present, and you hold your plans loosely so students can encounter God in their own way.

Sometimes you go off script or away from your outline in order to follow and respond to your students.

The content you offer is free of fear or shame, and you acknowledge that it's okay to be wrong, have doubts, and not have it all figured out.

You insist on reciprocating and learning with students by listening, sharing, and exchanging ideas or questions.

Your posture is collaborative and collective: other voices are invited to participate and offer content, even if you don't agree with them.

Part of creating space for dialogue and authentic conversation means welcoming every question and any doubts alongside belief. How do we create space where students' questions about faith are given as much dignity and space as their professions of faith? Rather than being a failure of faith, doubt is a healthy and vital component of our students' spiritual lives.

By the way, it's okay if we don't have answers. Sometimes the best answer is: "I don't know. I wonder about that too. Let's look into it together. Isn't God mysterious?"

As we prepare to be with students and engage them in meaningful theological content, how are we hospitable to our own questions and anticipatory of theirs? It's terrifying to wonder about something that we've always taken for granted as certain.

We've got to become good question askers and invite students to ask questions of their own. Students' questions reveal their deepest desires and help them figure out what they believe and who they hope to become.

A few years ago, I chose to build my entire teaching curriculum around middle schoolers' questions and let it evolve along the way. As I followed their wonderings, I figured we'd be in closer proximity to things that actually mattered to them, the desires that make them who they are.

Each student got a stack of Post-Its, and we encouraged them to write down any questions that came to mind during our time together. No question was irrelevant or silly, and no one would laugh at them. We set aside a whole wall in the youth room where they could slap up their questions, and then my leaders and I gawked at them after the students left, trying to understand where their hearts had been during youth group so we could plan accordingly for next week.

Here is just a fraction of their Post-It wonderings:

How do you know if God is speaking to you? What if it's just you?

Is the whole world like a dollhouse globe to God?

Did God make death, or did the devil?

If you get shot and go to heaven, will you look like a zombie?

What happens to pets when they die?

Do you have scars in heaven?

Is heaven really up and hell down?

Why does God love God's enemies?

Is God a dude or a dudette?

Why doesn't God make it snow more often?

Do we have to brush and floss in heaven?

So is God the BEST artist ever?

If God loves us, why can't we see him?

Why did God make the tree of [the knowledge of] good and evil?

If God is all-powerful, why can't he at least stop some little bad things from happening, like stubbing your toe?

Why were there more miracles a long time ago?

What do angels look like? Do they have wings and halos?

If God loves people so much, why does he let them suffer?

Why is there a hell?

What happens when a baby dies?

Why does everyone make Jesus white?

Does everyone who doesn't believe in God go to hell?

How do you know God loves you?

Why would God have to have three of himself if he is everywhere? Couldn't he just get a mirror?

If you commit the most horrible thing, will God still love you?

How was God created?

Does God need anything?

If God loves us so much, why can't he just put a shield around us so bad people and things can't hurt us?

Why is there earth? Why can't we just go to heaven?

Can it rain in heaven? (I like rain.)

Did God mean to make the world like heaven before it got broken?

If we are not allowed to see God, how can we be made in his image?

Did Jesus look different when he was resurrected?

Why does God get upset when we are imperfect? He knew we would be that way.

Why do we pray even though God already knows what he's doing?

Is it possible that God is the same God from all other religions, too?

Do we go to the new earth after we go to heaven?

Is God a vegetarian?

Why doesn't God answer our questions?

Why would I ever need to come up with content that I think they should know when they're already wondering about such amazing things? The trick is to ask and give them an opportunity to contribute and collaborate in determining what content we engage together.

We speak ourselves into being through our questions and also through our statements. It's developmentally difficult to grasp a concept we can't articulate. This is why so many good teachers have their students make presentations on a certain subject or read their work out loud—so they will grasp the material at hand in a different way than if they just read it to themselves or wrote about it. This is called "sensory reprocessing," when we take what we've learned and translate it into a different medium that transforms or enhances the meaning. The language we develop about ourselves is just as formative as the experiences and questions that shape our particular identity.

Teenagers are still practicing language, which is why oftentimes external words resonate with them so profoundly. Certain lyrics, passages in a book, or quotes help them express their lives when they don't know what words to say. I spent the better part of early adolescence compiling a notebook full of famous quotes and pithy sayings about life that were absolutely precious to me, because they gave me words for my experience that I couldn't have found on my own.

This is how we present the Bible to young people, more often than not. We say: "Here! Here is a voice you can trust to give meaning to your experience!" And our students latch on in beautiful ways without understanding that their journey must continue toward finding their own language for their lives. Sometimes, it seems like we're forming whole generations of Christians who feel insecure about claiming anything true for themselves without adding scriptural parentheses at the end to justify their experiences. It's vital that we bless the process of searching for language, of trying on different words to see which ones fit us best, but only so far as these things help us develop our own voice and language to express our reality.[20]

We find ourselves in every story so we can understand ourselves better. There will never be too many coming-of-age stories because each generation latches on to the language of becoming in their own specific way, and these myths become a part of the language they use to describe who they are. The narratives we love are the ones that reflect our own story in a way that is meaningful to us. Our desire to become like another person or a character in a story is a powerful force of formation that we're not often aware of. When students want to be like a certain famous person, it's because they see their desires reflected back to them in the most successful and ideal way possible.

This is why young people love quizzes, and that's why it matters so much to them which sort of Disney Princess they are or what their spirit animal is. Part of figuring out who they are means finding ways for the world to reflect them back to themselves. Every little bit gives them more information to test and absorb into their understanding of who they are and how they fit in the world.

We get to create opportunities for students to practice speaking about their experiences, self-image, and faith so they become more and more the men and women God has created them to be, according to their good desires.

This sort of space can't simply be architected like a LEGO castle. We are a significant presence in creating the sort of space that encourages teens to figure out who they are in the context of conversation, doubt, and self-articulation. The posture we take can invite the authenticity that students crave or the shame that sends them running from faith.

Our role is to be faithfully present with our students as they figure out the way their desires shape their unique identities. We can't tell them the answer, since we don't know; but we can be with them and offer support along the way.

May we learn to affirm them wherever they're at. The worst thing we can do is shame a student who's trying to figure out who they are. There are too many people walking around with that wound. We don't have to fix them, solve their problems, tell them our opinions, or fill healthy silence with nervous banter. Instead, we can welcome God's presence, trusting that our students' good desires will draw them toward the kingdom and affirm that their story—every story—is a possible gospel story. Sometimes the most pastoral response in the world is to say: "Me too."

May we learn to discern with our students and remember that we haven't finished the great work of becoming ourselves, either. We get to ask questions, wonder with students, and facilitate conversations. Some of the best conversations I've had with students or small groups happened when I asked only two or three questions and then encouraged them to work things out for themselves. This is difficult, and it can cause anxiety for some of us who struggle to sit with uncertainty and ambiguity. I hope you'll practice this and see that the shaky places are where we figure out who we are, what we want, and what we believe. God is in the midst of every earnest discernment process.

Finally, may we learn to reflect back to our students the truth of how we have experienced them. This doesn't mean we need to come up with something profound to say, or that we should ever conjure something out of nowhere in the hope of manipulating a student a certain way. We have the privilege of authentically and wisely showing our students who they are becoming. It's as though we are a truth-telling mirror that loves them, helping them to see and articulate their true selves that are both beautiful and broken. We've all had incredible moments where someone has seen something true in us that we'd barely allowed ourselves to hope for, and then it turns out that it might be true—and it changes us forever. We are living the dream. We get to know students well enough to speak truth over them, remind them who they really are, and name what is lovely in them.

It is sacred work to help students become themselves. It is an honor to name another person, to speak God's love and truth into her life in a way that connects with her heart's desire. Maybe this is what the psalmist had in mind when he wrote about deep calling to deep (Psalm 42:7).

The church cares about these questions of identity because we care about the sort of people our students become.

The developmental task of identity formation should be at the forefront of our minds as we make calendars, evaluate or create curriculum, engage in conversation, and continue to build relationships with students: Who do we dream our students will become? What sort of people do you hope to graduate from your ministry? How do you hope to form the kids in your care?

Of course everyone becomes someone unique. The last thing we want is for everyone to look the same—or worse, to look just like us! But what we desire on their behalf is a great orienting question for us as we go about our youth ministry. It can be simple or complex; it all depends on the sort of person you are. Maybe you'd prefer to think about it in terms of a mission or vision statement. It's totally up to you.

I try to share my dream for our students with our whole community—parents, students, and volunteers—on a regular basis. I prefer the form of a benediction, blessing, or prayer:

> May you continue to become more and more the women and men that God has created you to be.
> May you find that God and your community love you dearly.
> May you hold faith and doubt in tension, and have curious, respectful conversations with people who are different than you.
> May you keep desiring that which is good, true,

beautiful, living, just, and loving.

And may you find meaningful ways to participate with the Spirit in the restoration of all things and the reality of the kingdom.

As we become more in tune with our good desires and learn how to articulate who we are, we become more real. Real is good, because real is where God dwells.

11
WANTED:
SOMEWHERE TO BELONG

Somewhere, at this very instant, a group of teenage friends are hanging out, and no one is speaking to each other. They aren't in a fight. If you asked, they'd say they love each other, they're best friends, or they're Facebook Official. Yet no one makes eye contact, and their faces glow blue as they stare at their phones. This can go on for hours, this isolated togetherness. They are sitting there, and at the same time they are beaming themselves across town, across the country, maybe even around the world. Increasingly, this is what "quality time" looks like for adolescents.

Relationships that take place in reality are risky. Developmentally, teenagers are practicing their identities, so it makes sense that they'd be drawn to mediums of communication that save them from potentially awkward immediacy. Instead, they send both the precious and the mundane out into the world via disembodied electronic signals, rather than be present with the whole selves that God gave them.

A text message can't demand anything from them, really, not in the way that eye contact can. It's much easier to harm each other when they aren't looking at each other's faces. On the other hand, it's much more difficult to feel a lasting sense of love and belonging, even if they are drowning in texts, because you never know what a virtual friend will do in real life.

Teenagers have a deep desire for belonging, connection, and community. They don't retreat to screens because they don't care about one another or because they're lazy, antisocial, or awkward. They retreat for fear that this most precious of desires will go unfulfilled. Young people fear they want too much. Many can't imagine actually finding the community they long for. They wouldn't dare to hope, let alone articulate, their innermost desire for belonging, so they just keep looking or they settle for whatever they can get.

So as C. S. Lewis, the patron saint of desire, is infamous for suggesting:

> If we consider the unblushing promises of reward and the staggering nature of the rewards promised in the Gospels, it would seem that Our Lord finds our desires not too strong, but too weak. We are half-hearted creatures, fooling about with drink and sex and ambition when infinite joy is offered us, like an ignorant child who wants to go on making mud pies in a slum because he cannot imagine what is meant by the offer of a holiday at the sea. We are far too easily pleased.[21]

I wonder if youth ministry has been far too easily pleased in the realm of community, too. Thousands and thousands of words have been written about relational youth ministry, community, and helping people to generally like other people. *Community* is probably one of the top five buzzwords that most of us would use to describe our work with students.

What do you think of when you hear that word, *community*?

Unconditional love
Doing life together
Meeting students where they're at
Intergenerational ministry
Small groups
Incarnational-relational ministry

So much good has come from these words.

And yet I fear that sometimes we stop short of helping students be present with each other in meaningful ways, so they'll learn how to love one another and become more real together.

It's easy for youth group or church to become a belonging destination, like an all-inclusive love resort that we attend once a week, instead of a place where students have authentic encounters with themselves, others, and God.

The most common way of explaining our love for students is to point beyond ourselves to the fact that God loves them, so of course we love them. That's our job: to show them God's love for them. This is meant to be wonderful, reassuring news.

I have to confess that this response has always disappointed me. It isn't encouraging to hear someone loves me only because God tells them to do so, and he or she is able to say "the L word" without even knowing me. I don't trust this, nor does it connect with my desire to be known and loved. It's not unpleasant, but it's watery and rolls right off me like I'm a duck.

This is the same reaction I get after one of Ian's bike races, when I'm cheering on his friends who worked really hard but still didn't win. Yet there I am telling them, "Good job! Yay you! You rode your bike!" They look at me like I'm an idiot. My words mean nothing because I have no idea what I'm talking about, and they know it. So now I just say, "You didn't fall down! Yay!" It seems less idiotic to most of them.

Students aren't looking for a generic "I love you because Jesus loves you." They long to hear, "I love you because you are particularly, specifically lovable, and I believe God loves you because of you too."

Adolescents want more than blind love and acceptance from a community that's supposed to give it to them. They don't want to just be one more consumer of community; they want to be seen and loved just as they are and do the same for others. Usually this task falls to the youth pastor or other adult volunteers, where we speak formational words to students during prayer or pick-up times, when the whole group isn't watching. But it's not healthy for the community's intimacy to rest in just one or a few select people who dole it out in choice moments of vulnerability or disaster.

The community that teenagers crave pushes us beyond this. The title for this chapter is "Wanted: Somewhere to Belong," and it was carefully chosen. The sort of relationships that form us most meaningfully into the men and women we're meant to be, happen in specific places along the way and through relationships that are physically embodied.

Our students (and many adults) do most of their interacting with others in disembodied technological formats:

Texting
Emailing
Liking
Commenting
Posting

Blogging
Tumblr-ing
Tweeting

It goes on and on. The technology may be different in a year, but the distance will be very much the same.

Advances in communication have allowed teenagers to be in relationship at arm's length. What was at one time immediate, messy, and vulnerable can now be controlled, calculated, and revised. There is now a cheat code for relationships, a workaround for the unpredictability of interacting with another human being in person: disconnection and delay. In these formats we can practice being whoever we want, rather than having to stutter through just being ourselves and saying whatever awkward thing comes to mind.

This is why we see the heartbreaking moments of teenagers hanging out together while glued to their smartphones. Any screen is better than feeling awkward, uncomfortable, or exposed. It is a new phenomenon in human history that young people are able to avoid formational social experiences so often and so thoroughly.

Maslow's hierarchy of needs ranks intimate human relationships as the next most important thing after one's physiological and minimal safety needs are met. Once we know we aren't going to die—because we're fed, watered, and sheltered—the next thing we need is love. We need each other for the basic functions of survival—how much more so for love and self-actualization? And love can't happen when we're by ourselves; we need other people for that. Relationships are literally the foundation of being alive.

When we belong, we feel loved; and in the course of belonging, we learn how to love others. This is important formational territory for our students, and one of the beautiful ways we can support them in their development is by creating space for them to connect with others in a meaningful, tangible way.

It doesn't help that our theology prefers to be disembodied. Think about it. We communicate to our students that we can't touch the spiritual life, our souls are the most important parts of us in relating to God, heaven is a spiritual destination, and this earth will ultimately be blown to smithereens (so no need to bother with recycling that can because it won't matter in the end anyway). By separating our spirits from our bodies, we've done more harm than we can imagine.

The Hebrew language doesn't even acknowledge a separation between the spiritual life and the rest of life. A rabbi like Jesus would not have had a framework for what we mean when we ask, "How's your spiritual life?" because they believed that *all* of life was spiritual. Over and over throughout the arc of redemptive history, God calls us to wholeness—to find shalom between our bodies and souls, and to affirm that our bodies are deeply spiritual and that our spirits long to be embodied.

The thing about community is that it's not just spiritual or relational; it's physical. It demands regular doses of proximity. Our ministry is relationally anemic if we don't help students inhabit their community, rather than just coming to youth group once a week. To respond to students' desire for belonging means inviting them to inhabit their own bodies, to be present to each other in time and space, and to do the hard work of becoming together in all of our awkward glory.

My first gospel story, growing up in a non-Christian home, was *The Velveteen Rabbit*. Once upon a time at Christmas, a boy unwrapped a plush Velveteen Rabbit. He loved it until he got distracted by other things, and the Rabbit was forgotten among the many toys of the nursery. Except for the old Rocking Horse, the other toys looked down on the Rabbit because he wasn't mechanical. Soon the Horse and the Rabbit became good friends. Having lived in the nursery longer than any other toy, the Horse was wise in the ways of the world and knew the others would never be more than toys to the little boy.

"What is REAL?" asked the Rabbit one day, when they were lying side by side near the nursery fender, before Nana came to tidy the room. "Does it mean having things that buzz inside you and a stick-out handle?"

"Real isn't how you are made," said the Skin Horse. "It's a thing that happens to you. When a child loves you for a long, long time, not just to play with, but REALLY loves you, then you become Real."

"Does it hurt?" asked the Rabbit.

"Sometimes," said the Skin Horse, for he was always truthful. "When you are Real you don't mind being hurt."

"Does it happen all at once, like being wound up," he asked, "or bit by bit?"

"It doesn't happen all at once," said the Skin Horse. "You become. It takes a long time. That's why it doesn't often happen to people who break easily, or have sharp edges, or who have to be carefully kept. Generally, by the time you are Real, most of your hair has been loved off, and your eyes drop out and you get loose in the joints and very shabby. But these things don't matter at all, because once you are Real you can't be ugly, except to people who don't understand."

"I suppose *you* are real?" said the Rabbit. And then he wished he had not said it, for he thought the Skin Horse might be sensitive. But the Skin Horse only smiled.

"The Boy's Uncle made me Real," he said. "That was a great many years ago; but once you are Real you can't become unreal again. It lasts for always."

The Rabbit sighed. He thought it would be a long time before this magic called Real happened to him. He longed to become Real, to know what it felt like; and yet the idea of growing shabby and losing his eyes and whiskers was rather sad. He wished that he could become it without these uncomfortable things happening to him.[22]

Can you hear the gospel? This story drips with good news because it speaks to the hope that one day we will be whole and real. Almost everyone, whatever their religious beliefs, can relate to this feeling that something about life and the world is incomplete, that somehow we were created for a different sort of reality that doesn't include brokenness or shame or loneliness. There is a sense, which we can barely grasp with reason or logic, that the spiritual life is a way of longing for something more, something real, and that it's connected to the work of Jesus and the emerging reality of the kingdom here and now. We need each other in order to practice love and become real.

Community created reality. In the beginning the Creator, Son, and Holy Spirit collaborated to sing the world into being. Out of nothing, perfect community and love made everything real.

Humans were made to be in relationship with each other because we are created in the image of the original divine community. We become our individual selves as we become ourselves *together*. We want so badly to belong in community because learning how to love and be loved is how we become more real.

Each person has the capacity to reveal God to the world in a way no one else ever has, or can, or will—remember? We need to be with each other in order to know what God looks like.

Even Scripture can be understood only as we read it in community. By ourselves, all we read is our own story, our own politics, our own theology. Together, there's a chance we'll catch the sweeping narrative of God's intimate involvement in human history. Scripture is composed in such a way that we need the continuous intervention and imagination of each generation who keep the Word and the faith. None of us come to this text alone; none of us holds a "biblical" understanding on our own because we are limited by our own context, values, and experiences.

The most common ways the Bible talks about God's relationship to humanity is physical, which is strange when referring to a God we can't touch directly. Yet over and over, God's presence is expressed through physical means: fire, pillars of cloud, water, wind, bread and wine, and human lives.

In the garden of Eden, God *walked with* Eve and Adam. (Genesis 3:8)
Somehow, mysteriously, God spoke *with* people.

The Israelites were instructed to raise a tent *in the midst* of their community where God could be their neighbor. (Exodus 25)

The temple was a place where God's glory *rested*. (Exodus 40)

John tells us the Word was made flesh in Jesus, and he *dwelt among us*. (John 1)

Where two or three are gathered, God is *present*. (Matthew 18:20)

Revelation envisions a city where God *lives with people*—part of a new heaven and a new earth. (Revelation 21)

There is something about with-ness that saves us. Community is profoundly, counterculturally physical.

There's a reason most human cultures throughout history have had some sort of place set aside for worship, for remembering the sacred, for encountering the holy. The world is sprinkled with sacred spaces because there is something about the tangible that makes us believe we are real and we can have a real experience of the divine.

People's most meaningful encounters with God are when God shows up in tangible ways. It makes sense, then, that our most meaningful experiences of each other would happen when we're near others. Barbara Brown Taylor writes:

> What we have most in common is not religion but humanity. I learned this from my religion, which also teaches me that encountering another human being is as close to God as I may ever get—in the eye-to-eye thing, the person-to-person thing—which is where God's Beloved has promised to show up . . . The point is to see the person standing right in front of me, who has no substitute, who can never be replaced, whose heart holds things for which there is no language, whose life is an unsolved mystery. The moment I turn that person into a character in my own story, the encounter is over. I have stopped being a human being and have become a fiction writer instead.[23]

I believe that when we speak about community, we mean more things than just liking each other, holding each other accountable to religious moral standards, or being together in a room in a generally cheerful way. Too often we weave a fiction of community with little friction, few demands, and only peripheral commitment. We tell the story of us, but oftentimes we don't really know who "us" is.

What happens to relationships when we intentionally seek each other's presence without agenda or preconception? I'm not suggesting a youth ministry commune or compound where we all have dreads and weave our own clothing, but I do suggest that we teach each other to unplug and find opportunities to practice actually seeing each other.

Can you remember the last time you felt truly seen? I mean particularly, specifically, you in all of your occasional grossness and loveliness?

Maybe a friend spoke words you didn't know you wanted to hear.
Perhaps your spouse responded with grace and kindness when you were ashamed of your failure to love.
Maybe a student or a parent affirmed your calling when you were paralyzed by doubt.

This is what Christian community imagines: that we see each other's faces, knowing both the color of the other person's eyes and the contours of her heart. We invite her whole life—the shiny, proud bits, and the parts that are still heavy with shame. We sacrifice our comfortable distance to move in close and embody the God of love.

This vulnerability might hurt. It will be deliciously exhausting and hilariously awkward. There's a chance it will make us shabby or lose our hair, but the trade-off is we get to become real, whole, and fully embodied people. We were made to be in the midst of each other. It's one of the ways we reflect how we're created in God's image, and how we can learn the most about what God is like as we see God's presence in each other's lives.

Perhaps the best news youth ministry can offer to students who desire to belong is helping them learn to be present with their whole selves, in person. We need to be with others to know ourselves, learn how to love, and participate in the restoration of all things. Good news is helping ground our students in real places with real people, so they can become more real themselves.

This isn't limited to youth group, church, or our home denomination. The quest for community can lead us to places where we're surrounded exclusively by those who look, think, and act as we do. As we seek to form students into whole people, we consider that they'll be followers of Jesus in the midst of a diverse neighborhood, school, and workplace.

If we believe that something of God's presence is found in everything that is good, true, beautiful, loving, and living, then inviting other voices—even voices we disagree with—into conversation and community becomes natural. So much of Christian community is rooted in the sort of fear that leads to isolation, as if opening ourselves up to the experiences and presence of others in our community will somehow compromise our faith.

Just the opposite is true. We compromise our faith by sequestering ourselves amongst those who simply reflect their identical selves back to us, like one of those infinity mirrors in a fun house that shows you a million reflections of yourself. We can never become whole in isolation, or by pretending the whole world agrees with us.

If we believe we must embody ourselves in a particular place, then all of the people who inhabit that place are part of the deal. So our students get to do the hard work of learning how to connect with those who are different than them. As they do, they become more whole and more themselves. Maybe this is what Solomon means when he talks about iron sharpening iron (Proverbs 27:17).

How do we help students learn to be a part of a community that isn't made up of others who look, believe, think, and act just like they do?

The name of the game is neighborhood collaboration. We invite other voices—even ones we don't agree with—into respectful dialogue about life and faith. We partner with other organizations in our community that are working to offer good, life-giving, and loving services to students. Working with others who want the same good things we do—even if they use different words to describe their mission—is a recipe for participating in the kingdom of God.

As we locate ourselves in a place, in our neighborhood, in the midst of our neighbors, we learn how to fulfill the basic command that Jesus taught: to love our neighbors as ourselves. With our neighbors, whether or not they are Christians, we have the opportunity to co-create restoration and redemption with each other and with God.

In this way we learn how to love; and as we learn to love, we become more real.

12
WANTED: SOMETHING TO DO

Teenagers crave liturgy.

Depending on your experience of liturgy, this might seem crazy because it's usually the *last* thing students want. They don't want all of that rote religious stuff, or to be told what to do, or to feel obligated to act in a certain way. Maybe we need to expand the way our imaginations think about liturgy.

Even as students desire to find out who they are and where they belong, they also desire to practice all of that becoming and participate in doing something meaningful. They want to do something that matters, which is what I mean by *liturgy*. We can tell adolescents want liturgy because in many ways, they've already created their own.

Most of our students are swamped. From dawn until the late hours of the evening, they push themselves, or are sometimes pushed by others, to be "on." Some are stressed about achieving, performing, meeting others' expectations, and how they're going to get into college. Others numb the voices of pressure and trade stress for apathy and depression. They create their own liturgies of meaning to make sense of their lives.

Anyone who spends time in a high school can see the choreographed movements that help students create meaning in their day:

> The cafeteria is carefully engineered for social interaction with patches that are intensely inviting or devastatingly awkward for each student. Each group of students has their own language, clothing, mission, and posture.

> Hallways are navigated with each student's particular desires in mind: whether they wish to be seen by all, move around unnoticed, goof off, connect with friends, or just do what they're supposed to do. They've developed their own particular way of going through the day—a personal liturgy.

> Sporting events have their own uniforms, cadence, call and response, mascots that demand allegiance, and rituals of adoration.

Teenagers are always being formed by something, and the somethings they do over and over again form a sort of liturgy that tell us what they desire most, where they find meaning, and what they worship.

Either way, as individuals or communities, the things we do shape who we are and who we will become. All religions know this about the human experience and have created ritualized habits that mark and form the daily lives of the faithful. We all understand that we need to teach meaning, to hone our doings so they make us the versions of ourselves that we desire, rather than the culmination of unintentionality and blur.

It takes practice to become a person.

Liturgy literally means, "the work of the people." It's a way of speaking about the things we do that make us who we are, because we're always being formed by how we act in the world.

All churches practice liturgy, even the most "low-church," informal communities that claim to be totally cutting-edge and seeker-sensitive and seemingly allergic to words like *liturgy*. Many of us immediately think of older men in robes, smoky cathedrals, chewy toasted-cardboard wafers, and solemnity.

The church I grew up in removed almost every identifying icon and image in our building so the presence of crosses wouldn't dissuade nonbelievers from participating as soon they walked through the door. It basically looked like a community college building, but there are all of these Christians inside. Surprise! Jesus loves you!

This is liturgy too.

What practices does your faith community engage in that form who you are as a people? How do you participate in the rhythms of life and worship together that make you who you are as a collective? These are sensory questions about how our bodies engage together in actions that are meaningful to what we believe.

What comes to mind when you consider the way your community practices faith together? Most often when we think of liturgy, we probably think about sacraments:

Communion
Baptism
Confession
Confirmation
Anointing the sick

Holy Orders or ordination
Marriage

Depending on your faith tradition, some of these might carry more weight than others. Sacraments carry a sense of holiness, specific acts that the church participates in, in order to connect ourselves to God in both common and special seasons of life.

As I stated earlier, I have very recently found a spiritual home in the Episcopal Church. We see sacraments as outward and visible signs of an inward and spiritual reality, evidence of what God is doing in the life of our community. The thing that identifies us as Episcopalians is not that we all believe the same things theologically, politically, or socially, but that we gather together each week to worship, and that worship centers around Communion. Worship is where we practice being people of the good news, anchored in remembering Jesus' life, death, resurrection, and ascension by physically eating bread and drinking wine together.

We have a phrase: *Lex Orandi, Lex Credendi*, which means, "the way you pray shapes what you believe." The way we bring our desires before God shapes what we believe and how we engage with the world around us. Liturgy and worship are how we rehearse the way we wish to be in our daily lives: that we celebrate, confess, pray, and eat together so the kingdom of God will be more and more on earth as it is in heaven.

Ted Loder wrote in *Guerrillas of Grace: Prayers for the Battle*—

> For at last I believe life itself is a prayer,
> and the prayers we say shape the lives we live,
> just as the lives we live shape the prayers we say;
> and it all shapes the kingdom which expresses itself in
> and among . . .

I hope these prayers help you to take some new territory, to liberate imaginatively some part of your life, my [sisters and brothers].[24]

At the end of the church service one Sunday, some little girls were playing in the water of our baptismal font. Someone had taught them that you dip two fingers in the water and then touch your forehead, your belly button, and your two shoulders to form the shape of the cross. I went over and joined them, thrilled that they're learning to practice in their bodies what they don't fully understand with their minds. It's beautiful because they're figuring out how faith feels in their bodies.

Liturgies and sacraments help us mark our lives with meaning. Often we use "faith" as a static noun rather than an active, living verb. If our faith is going to form us in meaningful ways, we must practice it, not possess it in a jar.

If our prayers are the ways we offer our desires to God, then our practices are the ways we manifest our good desires in the world we inhabit. It's a way of seeing the world through the lens of the kingdom, that beneath the surface of things is the reality, a remembering and a hope, that one day everything will be restored. We get to live into our hope and practice resurrection through our habits of faith.

My husband has instilled in me a love for stories of magical realism. This is a genre of literature and film that depicts "what happens when a highly detailed, realistic setting is invaded by something too strange to believe."[25] Our liturgies draw us into the mysterious, fantastic quality of reality that is saturated by the presence of God in everything good, true, beautiful, loving, and living.

Liturgy invites us to imagine a world in which the presence of God is mysteriously present and where the mundane is made sacred by desire and love. What we do is very telling about the sort of people we are and the sort of kingdom we're building. Teenagers love intrigue and are drawn to this element of liturgy that invites them to experience something they don't quite understand.

The part that's important to remember is not just the magic, but the realism. Culture has shifted in such a way that much of the worship culture the church cultivated in the sixties, seventies, and eighties no longer holds meaning for young people. Their experience is saturated with people and corporations trying to get their attention with more noise, more sex, more hollow promises of meaning. They are savvy to ulterior motives veiled in entertainment and performance, and it's made them tired.

> It is a culture searching for an authentic encounter with God, longing for depth and substance, craving quiet and spiritual contemplation and moved by visual, tactile forms of communication . . . They are much more likely to utilize liturgical elements than their predecessors. And they reject slick, tightly orchestrated programs that are more show than "real." The younger evangelicals are longing for an encounter with God's presence.[26]

The things we say or do over and over are the things that shape our identities and the lives we lead. Our habits shape who we are and offer insight into what or who we love the most. Spiritual formation or Christian education oriented around cognitive assent to doctrinal positions has very little impact on how students engage with the world.

As James K. A. Smith writes, "Liturgies—whether 'sacred' or 'secular'—shape and constitute our identities by forming our most fundamental desires and our most basic attunement to the world. In short, liturgies make us certain kinds of people, and what defines us is what we *love*."[27]

Further, the way we involve our bodies is essential to formation. Students, in particular, are active beings with a heightened awareness of their bodies. Their muscles are constantly committing movements to memory. The way to students' hearts is through their physical bodies because they cannot grasp things beyond the cognitive level. Stories, music, and images are attractive to young people because they communicate on a visceral, not a cerebral, level. James K. A. Smith writes, "Habits are inscribed in our heart through bodily practices and rituals that train the heart, as it were, to desire certain ends."[28]

Much of church life is marked by tangible symbols of intangible beliefs. The things that impact our senses stick with us. The seminary I attended goes through those red candies, Hot Tamales, like it's their job. Jars of them are placed in strategic spots of desperation throughout the building. Every term there is an accounting of how many pounds we consumed as a community.

I will never eat another Hot Tamale without thinking about my experience with the community of my school.

This is what Jesus was doing with Communion, I bet. He took this portion of the Passover meal, which was already a pretty memorable deal, and chose the most common elements of food and drink to be reminders of his life, death, and resurrection. In Communion we are invited to encounter God's presence in our most basic desires: food and drink.

Youth ministries can respond to adolescents' desire for something meaningful to do by being really intentional about the practices that define our communities. There is nothing too small to consider because everything forms us in some way. Everything good can invite us to mark the sacred and create meaning. By the way, this is why emphasizing formation in student ministry is vital, because there are about a million other voices vying for the chance to shape who students become, and not every voice serves life.

Liturgy is awkward. We adults, let alone our students, aren't used to naming things or noticing the meaning that we're making. But it gets less awkward with practice, and I find it helps everyone if we just admit how uncomfortable we all are and agree to jump in anyway.

For instance, our student ministry starts off each school year with a gathering of students and their parents where we reconnect, reflect on the previous year, share our hopes for what is ahead, and speak blessings to one another. Well, one day our students may be in a place where they're comfortable blessing their parents. For now, I alert parents ahead of time to the idea: I will create space in our gathering where they'll have an opportunity to speak words of hope, blessing, or prayer over their teenagers for the coming year. When students hear this is what we're about to do, you can almost hear their eyes roll as they frantically look at one another and then search for a way to escape. I tell them they can blame me for the awkwardness, but we don't get a lot of chances in life to speak truth to each other like this, so we're going to try it. Please bear with me and respect your family.

As a group we pray for the parents, acknowledging that they are a tremendous part of their teenagers' formation, and then we dismiss them into small family groups, pairs, or solo students paired with leaders who are prepared to bless them. For all the fear, anxiety, and avoidance that both kids and parents bring to this experience, it is part of our collective work, our liturgy, that has formed us into a certain kind of people. At the very least, once a year, students and parents know they will have a chance to speak gospel words to each other.

Some liturgies are rites of passage like this. Throughout the teenage years, most of the rites of passage that students look forward to are lacking in formation, with the exception of getting their driver's license. That one opens up whole worlds of possibility and becoming. Otherwise, they get to watch rated R movies, vote, smoke, and buy pornography. Welcome to adulthood.

There is space and necessity for us to creatively imagine ways to welcome students into our faith communities and into the neighborhood as adults. Otherwise life just passes us by. We have to go out of our way to call things good, sacred, and formational, or else we'll miss the chance to tap into young peoples' desire for meaning. Youth workers have the privilege of helping students mark their own lives and remember how they are formed in the image of God to be part of the restoration of all things.

What would it look like to bless students' lives with some sort of liturgy, or ritual, or rite of passage? It doesn't have to be magnificent or involved. Maybe before their final exams you could take them to a pond or a lake or a river. Using permanent markers, ask each student to write his or her biggest fear or stress or worry on a rock, and then chuck that rock as far as possible because it doesn't define them. We get to play with creating moments that matter, moments we can touch, feel, taste, hear, and remember in the midst of so much unexamined life.

Other work we do as a community is oriented around the different seasons of the year. Our lives have a cadence to them, and each month of the year brings a unique set of challenges and opportunities. One thing I like to do is think about where teenagers and parents will be each month—not how busy they will be physically, but what spiritual and emotional experiences they might be having. This has been an incredible help in planning the rhythm of our year together.

The liturgical calendar often matches up with where students and families are at during the course of the year, and I think it's wonderful and amazing how the tradition of the church over thousands of years has made space for the full spectrum of human emotion and experience through the seasons of Advent, Christmas, Epiphany, Lent, Easter, Pentecost, and Ordinary Time. These seasons help us tap into the desires we don't even know our souls have.

Advent helps us practice anticipation and waiting. Our souls resonate with how the world ached with hope before Jesus was born, how badly we want Emmanuel to come, and how much we crave a reason to rejoice. The days of winter are even short and dark to match our longing for the Light. If we practice Advent well, if we help our souls rehearse waiting each year, then how much more elated will we be when Jesus shows up at Christmas?

Epiphany is terribly underrated. It's the coming-of-age season where we mark Jesus' meeting with the Magi, his baptism in the Jordan, and his first miracle at the wedding in Cana. This time of year was made for youth ministry, for us to show how valuable and important it was for Jesus to become who he was, just as our students are in the midst of figuring out who they are.

Lent invites us to reflect on our lives and prepare for the events of Holy Week. Almost everyone immediately thinks about giving up something, but it's really a chance to create space for our souls to seek God, like spring-cleaning for our spirits. It's a season of pause, of minimizing distraction so we can focus on the things that matter most to us about our experience of God. We set aside time, as the days are now getting longer, to remember God in the midst of our awakening spring lives.

What an incredible opportunity to invite students to practice reflecting on their own lives and how they encounter God in the world.

Easter brings a wave of relief and hope that the good news we suspected all along turned out to be true. We get to help students navigate the places in their lives where they desire resurrection, where they feel like they're becoming made new, where they hope to be restored.

Pentecost is wild. Students get to encounter a God who is unpredictable and wants to partner with them to restore the world through the Spirit. Let them play with fire or explore what makes them feel most alive and most like themselves in the world—this is the work God invites them to do as part of the church community.

Ordinary Time is how we cope the rest of the time when life doesn't seem very special or specific. It's a season of rest, of figuring out how to be ourselves when God's presence isn't quite so obvious.

We also get to teach students about daily liturgies that are a little more personal and individual. Maybe your ministry or church values devotional time each day. Perhaps ever since that retreat last summer, a student has been carrying a rock that's supposed to remind him that he encountered God (or he hasn't done laundry in a while). We can be as creative as we'd like because there is potential meaning all around us.

Some students find it really helpful to use the regular rhythms of the school day to remember something true. Can you imagine what would happen to a student's soul if every time the bell rang for class, she breathed in deeply and prayed: "All will be well. And all will be well. All manner of things will be well." Maybe she'd become more whole, more at peace with herself and with whatever the day brings because she'd be confident that God is in her midst.

Beyond our own formation and growth as followers in the way of Jesus, the work we practice as a people has everything to do with participating in the restoration of the world. We aren't made to sit around and sing to each other, bless each other, encounter God together, and call it good. It *is* good, but its goodness is incomplete until we are the sort of community that invites others into the unfolding reality of the gospel beyond Sundays.

The good news can't be good unless we live it. Our liturgies don't do much at all for the people the world has forgotten, but they may form us into the sort of people who won't forget them. The point of our rituals is to ground us in a certain understanding of reality, where God is present and active in the world through the good desires of humanity that long for goodness, life, love, truth, and beauty.

13
STUDENTS OF DESIRE

Orienting ourselves and our work with students around desire is a posture and worldview that continues to unfold, putting us in the beautiful and sometimes awkward position of always learning, even as we teach. This book is an attempt to engage with a topic that is bigger than words and as complicated as human experience. It is written in pencil, and I truly can't wait to collaborate with the youth ministry community around fleshing out these concepts together.

As we cultivate a kingdom imagination and attune ourselves to the presence of the Spirit, we will be better equipped to call our students' desires good and show them how they point toward God.

If we truly believe "the earth is the LORD's and all that is in it" (Psalm 24:1) and there is no place we can flee from God's presence (Psalm 139:7), then we must offer students an understanding of God here and now. Our hope is that as youth workers and youth ministries we will learn to be awake, like Jacob, to God's presence in places and desires we didn't previously suspect (Genesis 28:16).

We hope students will begin to see that God is always present and that in the Christian life we are called to recognize that presence as the deepest reality. If the whole earth is full of God's presence, then truth is all over the place, and we can be a part of it.

Students whose desires have been connected to the way of Jesus, to participating in the kingdom, are likely to continue following Jesus and pursuing the kingdom beyond their youth group experience. This is good news for them, for youth workers, for the church, and for the world.

Students desire places and people where they belong. Being with others is just as important for their identity development and sense of self as processing these things on their own, and perhaps more so. Becoming is hard enough work with a place to belong, let alone without one. Students are navigating expectations and demands that assault them from within and from without; they experience destabilization in their fragile identities, and every self-doubt simply leads to more self-consciousness and doubt.

Youth ministry can offer students a place and relationships where they can be fully known and loved in safety. What is true, over and over again, is that we need other people to reflect to us who we are; people who help us remember ourselves and who don't ask that we lose ourselves in order to be loved. Mark Yaconelli writes that we create and teach students to foster a safe environment where love quiets the "demanding and accusing voices so that we can begin listening to quieter, deeper voices and begin to know who and how we really are."[29] Community also means encouraging students and adults in their commitment to each other and their desire to walk with each other through life in all of its glory and tragedy.

Engaging students in their desires can be a daunting task for any youth pastor because it requires us to be rooted in both the beauty and the brokenness of who we are, and to trust deeply in the ever-presence of the Holy Spirit to guide us. In the words of Parker J. Palmer, we seek to be teachers "who know how to respond, not merely with teaching techniques, but with a conception of truth grounded in a rigorous and demanding love."[30] This sort of loving response, in the midst of the student ministry community, opens up space for God's presence to be made known and for students to continue to become who they are.

And in the midst of their desire, we get to help students cultivate a kingdom imagination that opens up the possibility of becoming more and more the men and women they were created to be, such that their hearts actually race, they are brought to tears, or they are simply left speechless. Imagery of the kingdom resonates deep in the fibers of who we are, and it calls us into a space of hope for who we will become. This is spiritual formation, in a sense, but I am convinced that God is more concerned with bringing blessings out of curses and life out of death than with processes, prescriptions, and formulas for discipleship.

The gospel is still good news, and it can awaken within students a desire and an imagination for how God is at work here and now. With the church, we believe in the power of the story we're telling. Together we will read and tell stories that cultivate desire for the kingdom and inspire us to participate in bringing heaven to earth.

Through their good desires, questions, musings, experiences and playfulness, students will cultivate their awareness for God's presence and participate in the surprising places where the Spirit is tending to the kingdom all around them.

May we remember gently
That we are made to be like God.
May we bless our own goodness, love, and desire
As we bravely name
And generously woo
The goodness, love, and desires of our students
So that they may find, in their many wanting ways,
The faithful presence of God,
The good news of the gospel,
And the reality of the kingdom.

ENDNOTES

1. Irenaeus of Lyons, *Adversus Haereses* (or *Against Heresies* Book IV, (c. 180).

2. Just a few of their book titles include: *Almost Christian: What the Faith of Our Teenagers Is Telling the American Church* by Kenda Creasy Dean; *Soul Searching: The Religious and Spiritual Lives of American Teenagers* by Christian Smith and Melinda Lundquist Denton; *A Beautiful Mess: What's Right with Youth Ministry* by Mark Oestreicher; and *You Lost Me: Why Young Christians Are Leaving Church . . . and Rethinking Faith* by David Kinnaman.

3. David Kinnaman, *You Lost Me: Why Young Christians Are Leaving Church . . . and Rethinking Faith* (Grand Rapids, MI: Baker Books, 2011), 92–93.

4. C. S. Lewis, *The Voyage of the Dawn Treader* (New York: HarperCollins, 1994), 109.

5. The Episcopal Church, "Daily Morning Prayer: Rite Two, Confession of Sin," *The Book of Common Prayer* (New York: The Church Hymnal Corporation, 1979).

6. C. S. Lewis, *The Last Battle* (New York: HarperCollins, 2002), 205–206.

7. James K. A. Smith, *Desiring the Kingdom* (Grand Rapids, MI: Baker Academic, 2009), 39–40.

8. BBC, *Secrets of the Superbrands: Technology*, aired May 17, 2011, https://www.youtube.com/watch?v=Dce6pUaZzcw.

9. Suzanne Collins, *Mockingjay* (New York: Scholastic Press, 2010), 388.

10. Tina Fey, *Bossypants* (New York: Reagan Arthur Books, 2011), 173.

11. Bob Marley, "One Love," *One Love: The Very Best of Bob Marley and The Wailers* (Universal, 2005).

12. Taylor Swift, "Change," *Fearless* (Big Machine Records, 2008).

13. Hafiz, " I Know the Way You Can Get"
14. For those who don't know, Bob Ross was an American painter who hosted *The Joy of Painting* on PBS from 1983 to 1994.
15. Rob Bell, *Velvet Elvis: Repainting the Christian Faith* (Grand Rapids, MI: Zondervan, 2005), 91.
16. As sung in verse 3 of Isaac Watts' "When I Survey the Wondrous Cross": *See from His head, His hands, His feet / Sorrow and love flow mingled down! / Did e'er such love and sorrow meet / Or thorns compose so rich a crown?*
17. Based on a passage from *Teaching as a Subversive Activity*, by Neil Postman and Charles Weingartner (New York: Dell Publishing Co., 1969), 49.
18. *Teaching as a Subversive Activity*, 35–36.
19. *Bossypants*, 84–85.
20. An idea expressed by my friend Kristin Gilfillan during a conversation at Chocolati on September 25, 2013.
21. C. S. Lewis, *The Weight of Glory: And Other Addresses* (New York: HarperCollins, 2001), 26.
22. Margery Williams, *The Velveteen Rabbit* (New York: Avon Books, 1975), 12–13, 16.
23. Barbara Brown Taylor, *An Altar in the World: A Geography of Faith* (New York: HarperCollins, 2009), 102.
24. Ted Loder, *Guerillas of Grace: Prayers for the Battle* (Minneapolis, MN: Augsburg Fortress, 1981).
25. Matthew C. Strecher, "Magical Realism and the Search for Identity in the Fiction of Murakami Haruki," *Journal of Japanese Studies* 25, no. 2 (Summer 1999), 267.
26. Robert E. Webber, *The Younger Evangelicals: Facing the Challenges of the New World* (Grand Rapids, MI: Baker Books, 2002), 190–191.
27. James K. A. Smith, *Desiring the Kingdom* (Grand Rapids, MI: Baker Academic, 2009), 25.
28. Smith, 58.
29. Mark Yaconelli, *Growing Souls: Experiments in Contemplative Youth Ministry* (El Cajon, CA: Youth

Specialties, 2007), 140.
30. Parker J. Palmer, *To Know as We Are Known* (San Francisco: Harper, 1993), 46.